edroom
makeovers

Frances Halliday

MEREHURST

C o n t e n t s

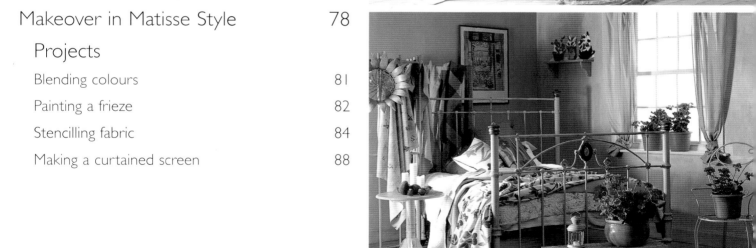

The bedroom is often the last room in the home to be decorated. And yet it is the one room where you can really express yourself. In this book, the same bedroom has been given six makeovers using a variety of colour schemes and painting styles to show you how different one room can look. Paint is inexpensive and offers an immediate way to update not only your walls but your floors, furniture and accessories too. Today's demand for colour has led to a huge growth in the range of paint colours available.

Colour is a wonderful tool; it can literally transform everything it touches, and it is a vital part of our lives. It affects us in a way that we cannot fully appreciate: it can induce a range of feelings within us, and can cause us to respond in ways that we do not understand. Colour can assist in making changes to our moods from happy to sad and from good to bad. Our unique ability to define differences in colour separates and distinguishes us from all other species. With so many magazines dedicated to homes and interiors, paint manufacturers are producing more and more colour ranges, giving us more colour choices than ever before.

This book should be used as a practical guide to selecting paints and colours for your bedroom. Discussion on colour theory will help you to choose and use colour in the home. Practical advice on paint products and their suitability for different surfaces is combined with inspirational examples showing the use of colour and its effect. The selection of projects

undertaken here can all be adapted to suit your own particular ideas for your own bedroom.

The colour schemes used in this book vary from fresh, bright lemon and lime to warm terracotta, and from moody blue to a riot of colour in the Matisse-style bedroom. In addition to flat painting of walls and woodwork, several paint effects are introduced. If you have been discouraged in the past from attempting paint effects because of the complicated process involved with oil paint, acrylic paints will be a welcome discovery. They can be adapted very easily and are available from most DIY stores. Acrylic varnish was also used to create several of the room makeovers. The process of mixing small quantities of emulsion paint with acrylic varnish is very easy and it allows you to experiment with different forms of application.

All the paint effects and techniques shown throughout this book can be used in many different colours and styles. Experiment first and try out your ideas on lining paper or off-cuts of wood. Keep these in your bedroom for a few days and see how they change throughout the day in the different light levels.

In these makeovers colour is not only enjoyed in paint but also in other elements such as fabric and wallpaper. The individual projects allow as much or as little of that particular look to be re-created. With information on preparation and basic techniques, an absolute beginner to home decoration can have the confidence to put these ideas into practice. Everything you need to know to get started is contained within these projects.

Use these colour schemes and project ideas to give your bedroom a new lease of life; after all, there is no excuse for putting up with decor you don't like. And an advantage of experimenting with paint and colour is that if you don't like the finished result, you can repaint the surface and start again. The tremendous sense of achievement one experiences when looking at the end result is very pleasurable.

Using colour in your bedroom

Colour is one of the most wonderful and versatile tools of interior decoration. With the use of paint you can transform the darkest room into a light, bright space, or the loudest decor into a muted paradise of sophistication. Knowing how to mix and use colour is crucial to the success of any interior. However, because colour is essentially an abstract concept, many people find it difficult and bewildering to fathom. This lack of confidence is largely due to an ignorance of the basic principles of colour. In colour theory, as with most things, there are certain rules and guidelines that should be followed. As your confidence grows, you can even try to break a few.

THE COLOUR WHEEL

The colour wheel offers one of the most important ways to understand colour. It is a simplified version of the spectrum: circular in shape, it is an arrangement of the primary colours of red, yellow and blue, and the secondary colours of orange, green and violet. From these colours,

Colour can be used to change the shape and size of a room. Rich colours like terracotta diminish the space and create a warm dramatic environment. Cool blue creates an airy quality which can be accentuated by accessories in contrasting colours. Soft pastel colours blend together for a calming environment. Colour can also be applied to a divided space for interest.

all other colours are made, including greys, browns and neutrals.

Primary colours are equidistant on the colour wheel. A primary colour cannot be made by mixing any other colours. These primary colours can be mixed together in varying proportions to produce every other colour in the spectrum. When two primary colours are mixed together in equal quantities they produce a secondary colour, for example, when blue and yellow are mixed they create green; when yellow and red are mixed they create orange; while when red and blue are mixed they produce violet.

A tertiary colour is made by mixing an equal amount of a primary colour with the secondary colour next to it on the colour wheel. By adjusting the proportions of the primary or secondary colours you can create a wide range of subtle colours.

There are two basic ways in which colours react with one another: they will either harmonize or contrast. This is easy to see on the colour wheel: colours that harmonize are close to each other while those that contrast are placed far apart. If you wish to use colours that harmonize, choose a section of the colour wheel and work with just those colours that are adjacent to one another, for example blue with blue/green or blue with blue/violet.

The colours situated opposite one another on the colour wheel are known as complementary colours. There are three main sets of complementary colours: red and green, blue and orange, and yellow and violet. When two colours of the same tone and intensity are used in a room they will intensify each other, causing the eye to jump rapidly from one colour to the other, thus giving a shimmering effect. When opposite colours meet they create impact. They enhance each other and produce a vibrant visual sensation; each colour will appear brighter against its neighbour than it would alone. For example, green and red can work well together in a room when used in the right proportions; equal amounts of each colour can result in a jarring shimmering effect, but small hints of red in a predominantly green room can be very exciting. It is sometimes better to use near or split complementaries, for example, turquoise and pink, as used in the Matisse room (see page 78). In this room, highlights of red, green, purple and orange were used in the accessories to emulate the busy vitality of a Matisse painting.

The use of one warm colour alongside a cool one helps to create a feeling of balance within a room. Colours are either warm or cool. The warm colours are those that fall within the yellow-orange-red sections of the colour wheel while the cool colours range through the purple-blue-green segments.

COLOUR AND MOOD

One of the most important aspects of colour is that it is emotive; it stimulates all the senses, not just the eyes. Colour can be used to suggest and to accentuate the mood of a room as well as create an emotional response from the viewer. It can trigger a flow of images, emotions and sounds. Blue makes us think of sky and sea, mountains and streams. Depending on the colour and tone used, it can denote freshness and lightness or melancholy and alienation. Yellow is the colour that conjures up images of sun and flowers but it can also be harsh and acidic. It is therefore

vital that the correct colour and tone is chosen.

TONALITY

When choosing a colour, it is important to consider the depth of tone you desire. The tonal value of any colour will change with the effect of light. The more a surface faces away from the source of light the darker it will become. The framework of light and dark

The colour wheel below shows a simplified version of the spectrum with the primary colours of red, yellow and blue, and the secondary colours of orange, green and violet. From these colours, all other colours are made.

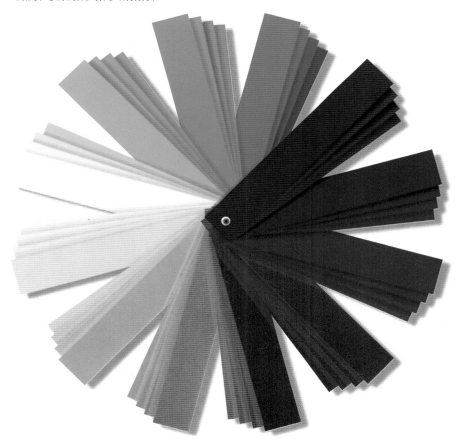

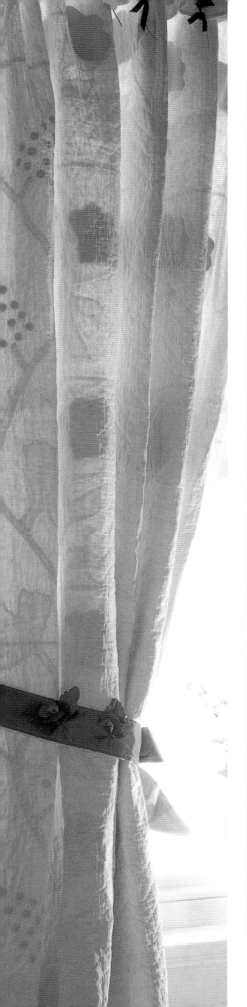

PINK

Pink is an extraordinary colour. It can range from pale candyfloss, through sugar-almond pink to subtle salmon. Pink works well with turquoise, its complementary colour and with the colours on either side of it on the colour wheel, violet and red. Psychologists believe that to sleep in a pink room will leave you in a good optimistic frame of mind.

areas that make up a room is often what initially attracts attention and will give an immediate introduction to the mood or atmosphere of a room. Tones and colours are modified by adjoining colours; a colour that appears dark when next to a white wall may well seem to have a lighter tone when surrounded by other colours. Colours and tones should never be regarded in isolation, but in terms of how they relate to others around them. All colours and tones are influenced by neighbouring ones. When two colours are viewed side by side, the contrast between them is enhanced. Each touch of colour added to the room alters the relationship of the colours which are already there.

COLOUR HARMONY

Harmony is possibly the most subtle and evocative of all reactions between colours and can be used with great effect to create mood in a room. While contrast is dramatic and may emphasize a special feature or area of the room, harmony is gentle and easy on the eye. There is harmony between those hues which lie on the same section of the spectrum or colour wheel, for example between the yellow and green featured in the lemon and lime room (see page 38). This is a combination frequently found in nature in the harmony of a spring landscape. Although harmonious schemes are often the most pleasing and easy to achieve, the very qualities they possess that make them harmonious may also make them monotonous. So it is important to enliven the colour scheme with suggestions of complementary colour.

CHOOSING COLOURS

At an early age peer pressure can influence colour choice. For example, we are taught from an early age to see red for danger, black for sadness, white for innocence, pink for a girl and blue for a boy. Adults' colour preferences can be dramatically controlled by rules of conformity, society and by individual experiences.

Like everything else, paint colours are subject to fashion fads. Just as clothes designers change their colour range each year, so do the fabric and wallpaper design houses. This puts pressure on paint manufacturers to keep up with current trends. Thus, each year, more and more subtler shades are added to paint ranges. Consumers can only benefit from the wider choice, but it does make the task of choosing colours all the harder.

There are some colour combinations, however, which never seem to fall prey to fashion, and these go on evolving through the years, still managing to look new and exciting; blue and yellow, or the classic neutral

SOOTHING

AQUA

Aqua is a colour derived by the mixing together of blue and green. It is on the cooler side of the colour wheel, which means that it recedes in a room, creating the feeling of space and depth. Aqua is a versatile colour with a gentle cleansing ambience and, with its connotations of water, it creates a soothing atmosphere, perfect for the bedroom.

A P P L E

GREEN

Green is a good natural colour, varying in hue from citrus lime to sage, and is found on the cool side of the colour wheel. It can look dramatic when partnered by red or by orange. For a more harmonious combination, use blue and yellow. Green also works well with the pale natural range, like vanilla and linen.

range are obvious examples. But for some, the idea of using a colour that has been used before is not appealing; the yearning for originality and inspiration is too strong to suppress.

EFFECT OF LIGHTING

Before choosing colours for your bedroom, check the quality of natural light your room receives. In sunlight, colours usually take a stronger or deeper tone than in poor natural light. In a bedroom that has poor natural light you might do well to choose pale colours for your decorating scheme which will reflect light back into the room rather than absorb it. Determine the general direction from which the light is entering the room, as this may alter at different times of the day. A room which faces due south and so is a little dull in the mornings might induce you to brighten it up by painting the walls a sunny yellow; this could send you racing for your sunglasses in the afternoon when the room is flooded in natural sunlight. One solution is to opt for colours and tones which work well in both artificial and natural light.

CREATING ATMOSPHERE

Another aspect to consider is the atmosphere you want to create in your bedroom. Dark and warm colours can make a room cosy and more intimate, but they can also make the room appear smaller. Red, orange, yellow and pink are generally described as advancing colours, that is, they appear to come towards you when applied to the wall. Warm colours are good to use in cool north-facing rooms, as they provide a feeling of warmth and create cosy interiors. Light, cool colours, on the other hand, can create a feeling of space and airiness. Blue, white and green are cool colours; use them in a south-facing room to create a fresh, calm scheme.

All the room makeovers featured in this book have a strong individual atmosphere which was purposely created by the careful use of colour, furnishings and accessories. In the terracotta room, the atmosphere derived from the memory of a Greek holiday. In the Matisse room, a painting dictated the use of sunny colours and roughly painted walls.

Atmosphere is dependent not just on colour but on texture as well. When choosing paint, there are many options available in addition to emulsion: satin, gloss, eggshell and silk are all now available in acrylic water-based paint, as well as in oil paint. With the introduction of acrylic water-based varnish, glazes can be mixed up easily; these give an extra dimension of texture to a room when applied over plain white walls.

TRANQUIL
BLUE

True moody blue is a timeless favourite. It is the supreme cool colour, evoking a sense of tranquillity. Blue's rich and varied tones are endless. Deep intense blues can give an energetic and fresh feel to a room, adding depth and contrast. Pale, subtle and muted shades of blue can create the feel of open, airy spaces.

SUNSHINE

YELLOW

Yellow is the most cheerful of colours. Its bright light-reflecting quality cannot help but lift your spirits. Yellow is warm and will bring a source of light to even the darkest of rooms. Its tonal range travels from citrus lemon through to sultry yellow ochre, with sunny and muted shades in between. Yellow works well with blue, purple and green.

TESTING COLOURS

It is a good idea to do as much research as you can before actually commencing your decorating. If you intend to use a fabric either for blinds or curtains, then your colour choice should reflect that. Perhaps this could be your starting point or colour reference. Always take a small piece of your chosen fabric or wallpaper with you when choosing either paint or accessories; don't rely on your memory, as it will undoubtedly let you down. Try to access as many of the design houses as you can. Treat yourself to a few of the interior magazines readily available in newsagents. And when you feel that you have seen as much as you need to, go to your nearest paint supplier and collect a range of paint swatches. Don't be afraid to take as many different tones of your colour choice away with you as you like – they are there specifically for that purpose. Invariably the tones of colour will change in your own environment. Colour changes when it is compared to and against its opposite. For example green will look far greener when next to the redder tones. Blue will look more blue when it is next to pink as they harmonize together.

Try out a few of your chosen paint effects on sheets of lining paper. This will give you a realistic sense of the colour and the opportunity of perfecting the paint effect you are going to achieve. You can then pin these up in your bedroom and live with them for a while, observing how light changes the colour. Sometimes it is not the immediate impact that you desire; alternatively, the more subtle effect may merge too far into the background when lived with for a time. This will also offer you the opportunity to see how the light changes throughout the day. This may take time and will require patience, but it will help to create the look that is right for you.

EXISTING FURNITURE

Very few people are in the happy position of starting from scratch with an unlimited budget and no commitments to a few inherited heirlooms or granny's rosewood wardrobe. If you do have to work around inherited objects, do this in a positive way and make the room work around them. Perhaps you could use a colour indicated in a chair covering as the basis of your decorating scheme. If you really feel the need to change your decor and these items simply do not fit into the new colour scheme, there is always the possibility of re-upholstering, stripping or painting the pieces to match your room. Whatever you decide, don't ignore these items in your colour scheme, and pretend that they do not belong in your room, as the result will be one of incoherence and disappointment.

CALMING
LAVENDER

This beautiful atmospheric colour sits on the colour wheel between the two primary colours of blue and red. Because of the mix of warm and cool tones, there is a great balance within lavender's shade. You can either create a warm pinky lavender, or a violet tone, which will recede. Use it with green, pink or orange.

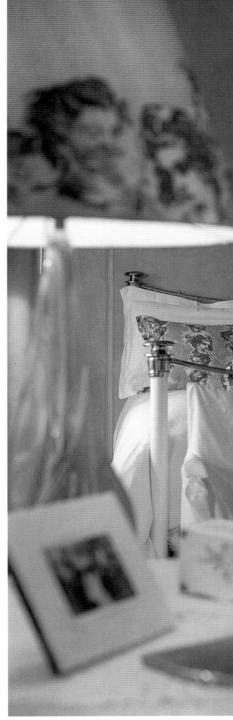

In the bedroom above a touch of lavender has been used in the accessories of a predominantly blue room to provide atmosphere. The touches of white offer a fresh contrast to the blue. A repeating image links accessories, thus unifying the room.

Paint Products

The selection of paints, varnishes and other products for decorating that are available can be confusing for a keen amateur. These pages will help you through the maze of products and guide you to the correct selection for the project you are undertaking and the surfaces on which you intend to apply it.

Paint is coloured pigment suspended in a medium which makes it spreadable and gives it an acceptable drying time. Paint also contains the relevant chemicals to ensure that it does not rub off easily and that the colour will not fade too much. It can be helpful to understand how paint is manufactured. There are two main processes involved: one for water-based paints and one for oil-based paints.

WATER-BASED PAINTS

Water-based paints are known as emulsion paints. They are water soluble and are made by pushing ground pigment (colour in its purest form) into a solution of water and polyvinyl acetate (PVA) resin. PVA is a type of plastic. The pigment is forced into the resin and water at such high speed that it breaks up and disperses evenly. When you apply a PVA paint to your walls you are effectively applying a skin of coloured plastic and water. The water evaporates and you are left with an even coating of coloured plastic. The greater the shine on the PVA paint, the higher the ratio of plastic to water.

OIL-BASED PAINTS

Oil-based paints, such as eggshell and gloss, are more complicated to make and as a result are more expensive to buy. You can expect oil-based paints to last much longer than many water-based ones. Oil-based paint is made by first making a 'binder', which is a mixture of linseed oil, acid and alcohol. To this are added some thinners (white spirit) and ground white pigment, and this is then mixed. The pigment does not break up and disperse during this process so the mixture is now ground in a mill to ensure that an evenly whitened paint base results. Finally, some more thinners are added, along with a chemical drier and some stainers. The product goes through a staining process before it is officially called paint. You may be familiar with paint base; this is the product to which the DIY stores add stainers in order to colour the paint to your requirements. So, when you apply oil-based paint you are simply covering your surface with coloured oils. As it contains all these chemicals you will understand why it smells so powerfully.

PRIMER

Primer can be either water or oil based. It is used on bare wood to seal the surface and prevent the wood from swelling when the undercoat and top coat are applied.

UNDERCOAT

Undercoat can be either water or oil based. It is a thin surface preparation and is used to seal walls and wood-work before the top coat. It has a matt finish.

VINYL MATT PAINT

Vinyl matt paint is practical and inexpensive to use for covering large areas quickly. As it is water based, it does not have an offensive smell and has no shine at all. Matt paints are difficult to wash if they become dirty but they can be touched up very quickly and easily.

VINYL SILK PAINT

Vinyl silk paint is much the same as vinyl matt paint but easier to clean if it gets dirty and has a slight shine to it. For creating paint techniques your base coat must have a slight shine so this type of paint is recommended in place of matt finishes. There are now some washable vinyl paints on the market which help to overcome the difficulties of keeping a surface which is matt-painted looking like new.

EGGSHELL PAINT

Oil-based or eggshell paint has a good satin shine to it and usually a greater intensity and lustre of colour. It is more expensive than vinyl paint but will last at least twice as long. Eggshell paint has an offensive smell and it is recommended that, when using it, you work in a well-ventilated area to prevent inhalation of the fumes. Eggshell paint takes longer to dry than water-based paints. However, the effect of oil-based paint on a surface is more professional than water-based paint.

GLOSS PAINT

Gloss paint is almost always oil based and has a full gleam to it. It is quite difficult to apply and should be brushed over a surface in two or three thin coats using a good-quality brush. Over time, the shine of the gloss will reduce and it will need repainting.

RADIATOR PAINT

Radiator paint has a lower quantity of ingredients which may yellow with heat. It also contains ingredients which prevent the paint peeling off a hot surface or softening when the radiators are on. Radiator paint is much more expensive to buy than other paints and the choice of colours is limited. If you are prepared to repaint your radiators as time goes by then you can use any shade of eggshell paint. Always work on a cold surface.

TILE PRIMERS

Tile primers are designed for those who cannot afford the luxury of new tiles when changing the room decor. You can safely and effectively paint over your old tiles for a new look. Apply tile primer in two coats, leaving at least 16 hours between each coat as it dries very slowly. When the primer is dry, you can paint the tiles in any colour you choose, using an eggshell paint for a long life.

UNIVERSAL STAINERS

This is a coloured stain in liquid form which can be added to water-based or oil-based paints in order to adjust the colour. It is available in traditional artist's colours. Try raw umber for 'dirtying' a colour. Avoid black unless you are seeking a greying effect; as it can be too artificial.

VARNISH

Varnish is just like paint but clear. Most varnish comes through the initial production stages as clear gloss. Silicon powders are added to make a satin or matt finish. These powders settle in the can and it is imperative to stir the varnish well before and regularly during use. Varnishes which claim to bring out the beauty of your wood may have some yellow colourants added to them. You can stain varnish very easily for your own use by stirring in some artist's colours. Use oil colours for polyurethane varnishes and acrylics for water-based varnishes.

Generally, the thinner the varnish, the easier it is to apply and the better will be the quality of your finished work. Before buying varnish, shake the cans and choose the ones in which the contents sound most like water. Very thick varnishes, such as yacht varnish, look good after only a couple of coats but the coats are very difficult and time consuming to apply. It is preferable to apply four or five coats of a thinner varnish for a smooth finish.

WOODSTAIN

Woodstain is most often used for colouring untreated or bare wood. It can be either water or spirit based. Woodstain soaks deep into the grain of the wood but is transparent so that the original grain will still show through. Apply the woodstain in generous quantities and wipe the surface with a soft cloth when dry. Woodstain does not actually protect raw wood and you must apply a coat of varnish or wax over the surface after colouring it for protection.

WAX

Wax offers an easy way to bring some protection and sheen to wood. Wax will nourish and protect most wooden surfaces and can be repaired and touched up easily. Beeswax is still one of the best wood polishes (and also smells very pleasant). All you need to do is apply the wax just like a floor polish, leave it to dry and then buff with a soft cloth. Re-apply wax on a surface from time to time as the sheen dulls.

Waxes containing colourants are also available; these will stain the wood as you go. You may need to carry out several applications of coloured wax before you achieve the colour shown on the can. For the initial treatment of wood with wax you may benefit from hiring a professional buffer, such as those used to polish cars.

GLAZE

Glaze is another medium which can be coloured for use in creating special paint effects such as ragging and dragging. In simple terms it makes the colour slippery and moveable. The glaze is applied with a paintbrush or roller and then, while it is still wet, it is manipulated with brushes, rags, plastic or anything you like. When the effect is achieved, the glaze is left to dry and the paint effect will last for as long as ordinary paints.

Glaze is available in oil- or water-based forms; the oil-based glaze has more lustre and depth to it. When using glaze, take care to complete an entire section in one rapid session as, if the glaze begins to dry at the edges, you will see a significant 'watermark' where the overlaps are. Stop in corners only, having brought the glazed section to a neat finish.

ENAMEL AND CRAFT PAINTS

These paints are sold in small quantities and are useful for small jobs, detailing and murals. Their colours are very intense. Most enamels do not need to be protected with varnish and will keep their colour for years. Craft paints, on the other hand, may be water based and might resist a surface which has been prepared in oils. Always buy the best craft paint you can afford. The colour in cheap craft paint can fade rapidly.

ARTIST'S OIL CRAYONS

These crayons are just like children's wax crayons except that they are oil based. They can be used for touching-up jobs and for drawing fine lines where a paintbrush may be too bold, heavy or difficult to handle. An oil crayon can be sharpened to a point just like a pencil, and the colour can also be thinned or smudged with the aid of white spirit.

PURE PIGMENT

Sold in powder form by art supply shops, pure pigment is the base of all the traditional colours on an artist's palette. The colour of pure pigment is the most intense available and it can be mixed into either oil- or water-based products. It is expensive but you only need a small amount as you will not use that much at a time.

LINSEED OIL

Linseed oil can be used to make your own transparent paints by mixing with artist's oil paints or pure pigments, a dash of white spirit and, very importantly, a few drops of driers. Use refined or boiled linseed oil to minimize the yellowing effect. Linseed oil does not dry without chemical help from driers.

DRIERS

These chemical additives can be added to oil paints to speed up the drying time. Be careful not to add too much; one teaspoon is sufficient for 1 litre (32 fl oz) of oil-based paint. Any more than this may affect the shine of the paint, and make it appear powdery. Driers are an essential part of any painter's kit.

WHITING

A white powder, made from chalk, which can be added to homemade linseed oil paint in order to make it less transparent. Mix the oil into the powder a little at a time to avoid lumps, rather than putting powder into the paint. Whiting can also be used to make ready-made paints go further, but will have a slight whitening effect. Thin with turpentine, white spirit or water, depending on the medium of your paint.

Troubleshooting

THE COLOUR IS WRONG

If you are not happy with the colour you have applied, you could repaint the room. Alternatively, if the colour you have applied is fairly pale or light, consider glazing over it using a simple paint technique such as colourwashing or ragging. Your base colour will be toned down by doing this but will still glow through the transparent glaze.

If the colour looks too dark you could try sponging one or two lighter colours on top. Your base colour will show through but the whole effect will become lighter and mottled. If you are using two or more colours for sponging, use the lightest colour last.

THE SHEEN IS WRONG

If the paint you have used either does not have as much shine as you would like, or is too shiny, there is a solution.

Buy some emulsion glaze with a gloss, eggshell or matt finish, whichever is required, and apply a single coat of this on to the dry paint surface. Emulsion glaze looks like milk when wet but dries clear.

THE PAINT IS WAXY

Careless preparation can often prevent oil-based paint from drying, or drying with a waxy feel. If you are painting on to a wooden surface you must first prime the surface. Primers provide not only a smooth surface on which to paint, but also a base on which the top colour will dry and cure fully. If you have overlooked priming the surface, wash the troubled paint away with plenty of white spirit and wire wool and start again on a primed surface.

If the paint is drying very slowly with a waxy feel to it then you have probably applied the coats too thickly. The surface of the paint is beginning to dry and cure and is sealing in the moisture underneath it. If you can, leave the paint for a week and see if it dries. If the paint does not dry, scrape it off, wash the wood with white spirit and wire wool and start again.

THE PRIMER IS NOT DRYING

This is a rare problem and is usually caused by the primer having been applied too thickly. Primer should be thin and soak into the new wood when applied, providing a smooth and even surface on which to apply the top colour. If the room in which you are working is damp you may also encounter problems with drying. Try heating the room with a dry heat and see if the primer dries. If it still does not dry, scrape off the offending primer and begin again.

PAINT HAS BEEN SPILT

Every painter's nightmare is to spill paint on the carpet. If the paint spill is small, leave it to dry without touching it at all. It can then be removed from the carpet pile with abrasive sandpaper. Water-based paint spills can be removed immediately by washing the area with plenty of water and blotting with clean rags. Larger oil-based spills will have to be washed with white spirit and then with soapy water. Before washing out a spill, remove all the paint you can by scraping from the outside of the spill inwards.

NOT ENOUGH PAINT

If you notice the potential disaster of your paint running out in good time you can stretch your paint by diluting it a little with the appropriate thinner and by making sure that you use every drop of the paint which you have soaked your rollers and brushes with rather than washing it away into the sink. Sometimes you can buy a small tester pot of emulsion colour to help with that last square metre. If you are working with a colour which you mixed for yourself, and which cannot be repeated, then one wall or section of your room will have to be painted in a harmonizing shade or colour.

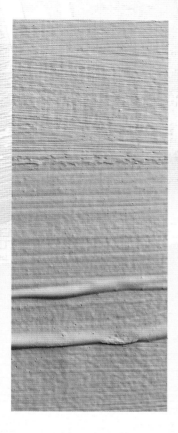

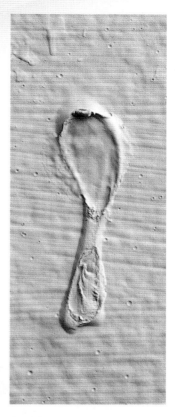

SAGGING

The paint has been applied too thickly or each coat has not been allowed to dry fully before the next was applied. To deal with sagging paint you must first allow it to dry fully and then rub the offending areas down with wet-and-dry sandpaper (use it wet for best results) until it is perfectly smooth. Now paint the rubbed-down parts again using the same number of coats as you have used on the whole area.

CISSING

This term is used to describe the appearance of paint which is resisting the surface on to which it is being applied and usually occurs when water-based paint, such as emulsion, is being applied on to oil-based paint. For large areas you will be forced to buy new paint in oil-based form. For smaller areas, try washing the surface with detergent and a light scouring pad to remove any grease which may be sitting on the surface. If the paint still resists, you will have to resort to using oil-based paint.

CRACKING

Cracking is caused when paint or varnish is applied over a base layer of paint or varnish of different elasticity before it has been given long enough to cure (which can take up to a month). For example, two separate brands of varnish may react with each other and form cracks. To deal with cracking you must allow the surface to dry fully and then rub it down ready for repainting. You could, however, consider leaving the cracking visible. It is a very popular ageing technique and many people seek this particular decorative effect.

DRIPS

Drips or 'nibs' in the dried paint surface are usually pure oversights before leaving paint to dry. Rub the dried drip away with fine sandpaper and repaint the area. On high-gloss finishes you may need to apply a final coat over the entire area to disguise the patch where you rubbed away a drip.

Product	Quality	Thinners and brush cleaning	Use for	Apply with
Primer	Preparation for bare wood. Prevents wood from swelling	Turpentine or water (check the can)	Bare wood	Brush or small roller
Undercoat	Matt finish, thin surface preparation and sealer	Water or turpentine (check the can)	Walls, woodwork	Brush
Vinyl matt	No shine, general-purpose coverage	Water	Walls, new plaster	Large brush or roller
Vinyl silk	Satin sheen, general-purpose coverage	Water	Walls, murals, base for glaze work. Not for new plaster	Large brush or roller
Eggshell	Satin sheen, general-purpose coverage	White spirit or turpentine	Walls, woodwork and metal	Large brush or roller
Gloss	High shine, durable	Turpentine or water (check the can)	Woodwork, doors	Good-quality brush
Woodstain	Colour without varnish for bare wood	Water or white spirit	Bare or unvarnished wood	Lint-free cloth or brush
Varnish - polyurethane	Oil-based wood and paintwork protection. Choice of shine	White spirit or turpentine	Wood and to protect paintwork	Good-quality brush
Varnish - acrylic	Fast-drying protection for wood and paintwork. Choice of sheen. Non-yellowing	Water	Wood and to protect paintwork	Brush or roller

Number of coats	Washable?	Area per litre (one coat) Square metres	Notes	Drying time pre re-coating	Drying time final coat	Undercoat
1	N/A	12 metres	Thin to a watery consistency. Rub down with sandpaper when dry	2–4 hours	N/A	No
1	N/A	12 metres	Stir well. Rub down with sandpaper when dry	Oil based – 8 hours. Water based – 2 hours	N/A	N/A
2	No	10 metres	Do not stir and avoid frost	1–2 hours	8 hours	No, but dilute first coat for raw wood
2	Yes, soapy water. Do not scrub	10 metres	Dark colours require 3 or more coats	1–2 hours	8 hours	Vinyl matt
2	Yes, house-hold cleaners. Avoid ammonia	15 metres	Stir well before and during use	8 hours	24 hours	Primer or commercial undercoat
2	Yes, house-hold cleaners. Avoid ammonia	12 metres	Slow to apply – use good-quality bristle brush. Oil based is more hardwearing	4–8 hours	24 hours	Primer
1 or 2	No	8 metres	Apply generously with brush or cloth. When dry, wipe off excess with dry cloth. Stainers do not protect wood; always wax or varnish when dry	1–3 hours	1–3 hours	No
Up to 8	Yes, soapy water	10 metres	Use thinned and apply several coats for the greatest lustre. May yellow as coats build up	4 hours	24 hours	No
Up to 8	Yes, but do not scrub	10 metres	Difficult to apply as evenly as polyurethane varnishes. Not as durable but quick drying and crystal clear. Do not use on oil-based paints	1 hour	8 hours	No

Product	Quality	Thinners and brush cleaning	Use for	Apply with
Wax	Protection and shine for wood	N/A	Bare or stained wood	Lint-free cloth
Oil-based glaze	Transparent	White spirit or turpentine	Mix with artist's oil colours to make coloured glaze for various paint finishes	Brush or roller
Craft paint	Intense colours for detailing and small areas	Various	Small craft projects	Soft brush
Artist's oil crayons and pastels	Intense, pure colours in stick form	Oil or turpentine	Detailing and drawing on walls, furniture or paper	N/A
Pigment	Intense colours	Water	Make homemade paints for colourwashing	Brush or roller
Car spray paint	Low or high sheen, hard-wearing, wide colour range	Cellulose thinners	Stencils and basic coverage	Spray from the can
Glass paint	Transparent or matt	Acetone	Painting glass of all kinds. Transparent detail work	Soft artist's brush
Blackboard paint	Matt black, very opaque	Methylated spirits	Interior matt finishes, chalk boards	Brush
PVA glue	General-purpose sealer	Water	Walls or woodwork to seal or stick	Brush

Number of coats	Washable?	Area per litre (one coat) Square metres	Notes	Drying time pre re-coating	Drying time final coat	Undercoat
3	Yes, with more wax or soapy water	8 square metres	Apply just like shoe polish, buff with a soft cloth between coats. Pure beeswax best for new wood; re-wax often	3 hours	N/A	Woodstain (optional)
1 or 2	No	Depends on consistency	Good workability for ½ hour. Cheap way to extend colour	6 hours	N/A	Oil-based eggshell base
1 or 2	Yes, do not scrub	N/A	Better quality than poster paints. Widely available in small quantities	½ hour	N/A	N/A
N/A	No	N/A	Allow to dry for 3 weeks or more before varnishing	N/A	N/A	N/A
1	Yes	N/A	Can be mixed with oil- or water-based products	N/A	N/A	N/A
1 or 2	Yes	N/A	Extremely hardwearing; wear a mask when spraying	1 hour	10 hours	Spray undercoat
1	Yes, do not scrub; check label	N/A	Brushstrokes always show up; beautiful vivid colour selection	1 hour	4 hours	No
1 or 2	Yes, water only	10 square metres	Fast drying, easy to repair and patch up	1 hour	4 hours	No
1	Yes, soapy water	12 square metres	Dilute 1:1 with water. Apply with brush	1–2 hours	N/A	No

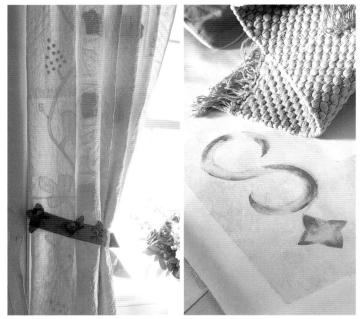

MAKEOVER PROJECT

Pastel Shades

These subtle pastel shades of raspberry pink, blue, lilac, vanilla and mint green complement one another beautifully and the combination of them is deliciously inspiring. The harmonious blend of light and air creates a peaceful and relaxed space.

There is a huge variety of ice cream colours to choose from for your room scheme. As these pastel colours have the same creamy and chalky hue, it is possible to use a large number of them in the same room. This is normally inadvisable as one colour can react against another, giving an

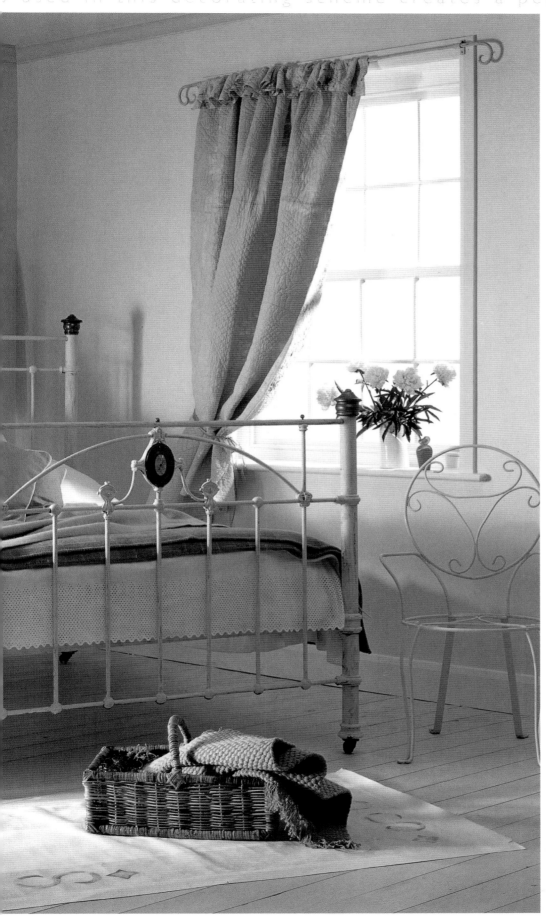

PROJECTS FROM THIS
MAKEOVER SHOW YOU

- HOW TO DRY-BRUSH A
  WALL

- HOW TO STENCIL A RUG

- HOW TO REVAMP AN
  IRON BED FRAME

- HOW TO MAKE A
  BEDSPREAD CURTAIN
  AND TIE BACK

overall inconsistency; however, in this case, the tonal range blends and shimmers together, with no one colour dominating, and each colour adding to the other's natural vibrance. The balance between warm and cool colours is broken only by the addition of accessories in slightly deeper tones; the furniture painted in a soft mid tone of lilac reaffirms the importance of colour equality. When using more than one colour in a room, give each colour the same amount of space. To create a balanced feel to the colour, you must use colours of similar intensity. The lack of pattern in the room helps to maintain the clean uncluttered feel.

PREPARATION

Make sure that all holes in the ceiling or walls are filled with general all-purpose filler, and that any loose wallpaper is stuck down fast with wallpaper paste. Any slight indentations will show up more after the surface is decorated. Protect any furnishings that cannot be removed with dust sheets; cover the floor, too, as splashes and drips will inevitably land there.

Mix the glazes, ensuring that you have the right amount required. You will need a clean mixing pail, acrylic varnish and a small quantity of the paint in the colour you want to apply. For each colour glaze you will need 1 part emulsion to 2 parts acrylic varnish. You can mix the glaze with a spatula; if, however, the quantity you require is great, use a paint paddle attached to an electric drill, to make mixing easier. Before applying glaze, mask off any adjoining surfaces with low-tack masking tape, as this will help to create clean lines.

DRY-BRUSHING

This technique is easy to achieve and results in a subtle broken paint effect which is perfect for pale paint colours, and also more suitable for this room scheme than a flat coat of emulsion paint.

EXPERT TIP
• *If the paint starts to flake when drying, it probably means that you have painted emulsion paint over an oil-based paint, such as gloss or distemper (see page 21 for the way to remedy this). Before painting with either acrylic or emulsion, always prepare the surface first by rubbing it down with sandpaper and applying a good coat of acrylic all-purpose primer.*

1 Using a household brush, apply a coat of vanilla emulsion paint over the surface to cover it entirely. Allow to dry.

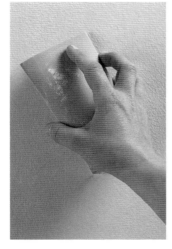

2 Wrap sandpaper around a block of wood and use this to rub over the painted surface. This smooths the surface in readiness for the top coat of paint.

3 Mix up a glaze with 1 part pink emulsion to 2 parts acrylic varnish. Dip a household brush in the glaze, then brush it over the surface in long vertical strokes. This effect allows the brushstrokes and part of the base coat to remain visible. Allow to dry.

Stencilling a rug

MATERIALS

canvas rug

low-tack masking
tape

emulsion paint: pink,
aqua

acrylic varnish

sponge

thick paper

craft knife

cutting mat

grey spray paint

stencil brush

gold paint

Painted floors can offer a great opportunity to match exactly the colour you are using on the walls, but they can be a little stark. Painting a rug in the same colours as the room softens the effect of the floor and unifies the room's colour scheme. This rug not only introduces the aqua used on the walls at floor level but it also echoes the swirl of the grey metal curtain pole.

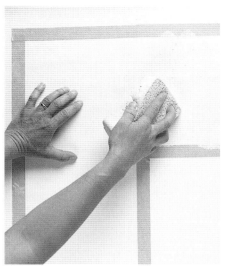

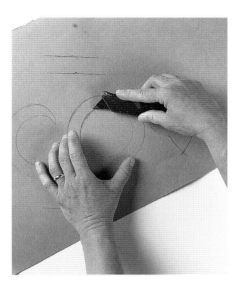

1 Stick strips of low-tack masking tape in a line around the edge of the canvas rug, about 5cm (2in) from the edge. Stick another line of tape around the rug, about 25cm (10in) in from the first line. This is to enable you to paint a straight-edged border around the rug.

2 Mix up some pink glaze with 1 part pink emulsion and 2 parts acrylic varnish. Lightly dab a sponge first into the glaze, then on to the masked-off border. Continue sponging pink glaze around the rug until the entire border is a soft mottled pink.

3 Draw a simple stencil design on to thick paper. This one reflects the design of the metal curtain pole. Place the paper on a cutting mat and, using a craft knife, carefully cut out the design.

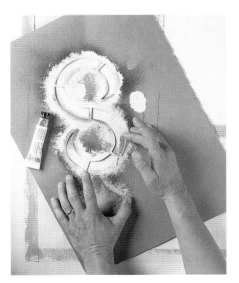

4 Position the stencil over the border of the canvas rug. Using grey spray paint, lightly spray through the stencil on to the border.

5 Keeping the stencil in position, stipple aqua paint through the stencil on top of the grey colour to give a more metallic feel. Allow some of the grey colour to show through.

6 Go over the stencilled motif with patches of gold paint, rubbing it on with a finger for an aged look. Continue to stencil in this way around the border of the rug. Then remove the masking tape to reveal the completed stencilled decoration. Allow the paint to dry thoroughly before using the rug.

Revamping an iron bed frame

MATERIALS

cast iron bed frame

bowl

rubber gloves

cloth or scrubbing brush

coarse-grade sandpaper

household paintbrush

all-purpose acrylic primer or anti-rust primer

emulsion paint: white, pink, pistachio

fine artist's brush

soft cloth

medium-grade sandpaper

raw umber paint pigment

acrylic varnish

dragging brush

silver metallic paint

You might think that it is all very well being tempted to buy an old jug from a junk shop, because you know that prior to it taking up pride of place on your dresser it will meet with a thorough wash or a keen dusting down. However, if the piece you intend to purchase is likely to be the weight of a small cart horse and rusty with it, the idea of cleaning such a large object might not be so appealing. However, this project shows that with a little determination and some elbow grease, it is quite possible to rescue and revamp a large cast iron bed frame, thus combining the elegance of an age gone by with the comfort and convenience of today's lifestyle.

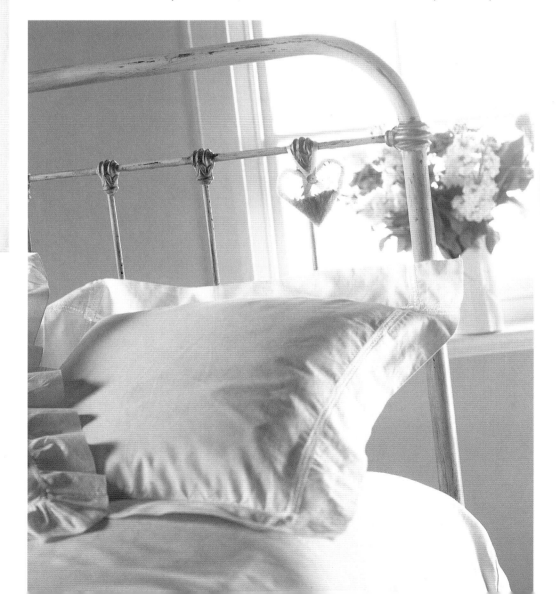

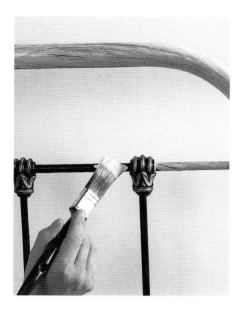

1 Before being able to tackle the rot or damage to a cast iron bed frame you need to remove all the surface dust and dirt. Fill a large bowl with warm soapy water and use a cloth to wash away as much of the loose paintwork as you can; alternatively, a stiff scrubbing brush will help with this.

2 Allow the bed frame to dry, then rub it vigorously with coarse-grade sandpaper to remove any remaining rust and old paintwork.

3 Using a household paintbrush, apply a coat of all-purpose acrylic primer over the entire bed frame. Alternatively, if there is rust present on the frame, use anti-rust primer instead. Allow to dry.

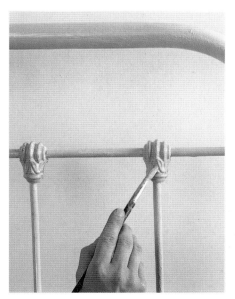

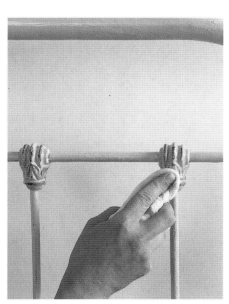

4 Paint a coat of white emulsion paint over the whole bed frame, watching out for any runs or drips. Leave to dry, then apply a second coat if necessary for an even all-over coverage.

5 Using a fine artist's brush, paint any details or features of the bed in pink emulsion paint.

6 Using a soft cloth, rub away some of the paint on the details to create the look of wear and tear.

7 Paint fine lines of pistachio-coloured emulsion paint over the details to highlight the intricate metalwork. Allow the paint to dry thoroughly.

8 Using medium-grade sandpaper, rub down the paintwork on the bed frame to reveal patches of previous paint layers, and in some areas bare metal. This will add to the aged and worn feel that an old bed would almost certainly have.

9 Make some ageing glaze by mixing a tablespoon of raw umber paint pigment in a pot of acrylic varnish. Brush a coat of ageing glaze over the frame using a long-haired soft dragging brush. Allow the glaze to pool in some areas, but do not allow any runs to occur.

10 Using a fine artist's brush, apply silver metallic paint to any intricate mouldings to highlight and accentuate these areas. Allow to dry.

EXPERT TIPS

• *It is a good idea to wear rubber gloves for protection when scrubbing down the bed frame.*

• *Although it is fun to use colour on an old bed, it is probably best to confine its use to very small areas and to tone it down with the use of ageing glaze if the bed is to have any real authenticity. Bright colours can look too garish on an old bed.*

• *Dress a cast iron bed with antique or reproduction lace sheets and large square lace-edged pillows, or use an antique patchwork quilt as a bedspread, combined with an array of different-sized and patterned cushions.*

Bedspread curtain and tie back

In this project, a simple curtain is created from a bedspread, while ribbons and silk flowers, normally seen adorning hats on high days and holidays, are used in an unusual decoration for a curtain tie back. In this pale room, which is continually flooded with light, the window dressing needed to be simple but also to exclude light. The solution came in the shape of a soft quilted antique bedspread which was double-sided with padding in between, therefore negating the need to line or inter-line. The bedspread was cream on one side and a soft pink appliqué on the other, so when the top was folded over to create a loop to feed on to the curtain pole, there was an instant design. A simple ribbon tie back to hold back the quilt curtain for daytime use allows a glimpse of the decorative silk flowers.

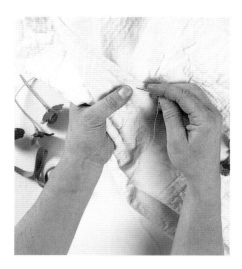

1 Fold over the top of the bedspread to make a loop of fabric that the curtain pole can be slipped through. Baste the fabric layers then machine stitch to secure. At measured intervals, handstitch the silk flowers and ribbons to the bedspread top.

2 Calculate the length of tie back you will need. Measure the distance from where you will position the hook on the wall around the curtain and back to the hook again. Then cut the length of ribbon accordingly. If your chosen ribbon is thin, back it with a more robust one. Lay the ribbon flat and pin the narrower ribbon on the top and machine sew around the edge. Tie a large bow in the centre of the ribbon. Stitch the silk flowers into position on one side of the ribbon.

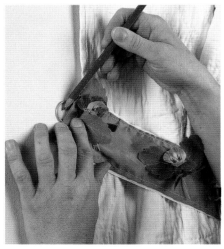

3 Attach a brass ring to each side of the tie back. Fold each ribbon end by 12mm (½in). Lay the ring on the folded end, fold back the ribbon to enclose the ring. Then stitch the ribbon to secure.

4 Position the tie back around the curtain and mark with a pencil cross on the wall the position of the tie back hook. Using a bradawl, make a small dent in the wall in the centre of the cross.

5 Attach the hanging hook to the wall by carefully tapping a nail through the hole in the hook. Then simply slip the tie back rings over the hook to hold back the curtain.

MAKEOVER PROJECT

Lemon'n Lime

This sunny colour scheme of lemon and lime is fresh, clean, youthful and invigorating. In this bedroom, you will want to leap out of bed in the mornings, full of vitality and enthusiasm for the day ahead.

Although paint has miraculous transforming abilities, sometimes the desire to use a much-loved wallpaper is just too tempting, and this combination of lemon and lime checks has always been a favourite. Many home decorators are reluctant to attempt to hang their own wallpaper.

PROJECTS FROM THIS MAKEOVER SHOW YOU

- HOW TO PREPARE AND HANG WALLPAPER

- HOW TO DECORATE WITH WALLPAPER

- HOW TO MAKE FROSTED GLASSES

- HOW TO MAKE A CUSHION WITH TIES

- HOW TO PAINT A PICTURE FRAME

But if care is taken and a methodical approach is followed, there is no reason why anyone should be discouraged.

In this room two different colourways of the same wallpaper were used. The checked paper is available in lemon and lime: the lemon was used on the ceiling and the lime on the walls. The cornice was dragged in a deep lime green and the woodwork was painted in turquoise. The window and door mouldings were painted light lime green. The bed was dragged in pale lemon and the table and clothes dryer were painted turquoise. The accessories picked up on the checks and lemon and lime scheme.

PREPARATION

Before wallpapering your room, remove the old wallpaper and make good any damage done to the wall surface in so doing. Treat any damp patches, as failure to deal with it at this stage will be expensive if the staining appears later through the new wallpaper.

Paste lining paper on the walls prior to hanging wallpaper. This should be pasted on horizontally rather than vertically; the effect of this is that it evens out any odd lumps and bulges in the wall, and prevents them showing through the wallpaper for an uneven finish.

HANGING WALLPAPER

Take your time when hanging wallpaper for the first time. Although it may look easy, achieving a neat finish with patterns matching and no trapped air bubbles takes a bit of planning and care. Unroll the wallpaper and measure out your required length; do not underestimate the drop. If you intend to use striped wallpaper, it is crucial that the first piece is hung vertically straight.

EXPERT TIPS

• *When papering around an arch, trim, cut and then fold the paper over to fit around the curve. Use a final strip of wallpaper to disguise the flaps.*

• *Scaffold boards suspended between stepladders will give you a safe and sturdy base from which to reach ceilings and inaccessible corners.*

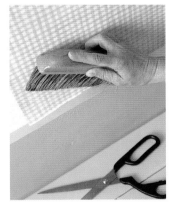

1 Ensure that the wallpaper pattern is both vertically and horizontally correct. Brush wallpaper paste over the back of the wallpaper. Place the wallpaper on to the prepared wall surface. Then, using a dry, clean brush and applying gentle downward pressure, stroke the wallpaper smoothly into position. Brush out any air bubbles that are trapped between the wall and the paper.

2 Where the wallpaper meets and overhangs the skirting board, gently push the wallpaper into the corner to make a neat, straight fold. Using the wallpaper shears, carefully score along the folded edge to enable you to trim away the excess wallpaper.

3 Gently peel back the wallpaper at the base and, using the shears, cut cleanly along the scored line. Take care not to leave any ragged edges or rip the paper. Either discard the excess wallpaper, or put it to one side for making wallpaper scallops (see page 42).

4 Using the dry papering brush, push the wallpaper back against the wall. Gently scrub the paper into the corner with the edge of the brush. Using a soft damp cloth, wipe away any residue of paste that may be left on either the wallpaper or the skirting board.

MATERIALS

dinner plate

wallpaper

masking tape

pencil

cutting mat or
cardboard

craft knife

saucer

pinking shears

wallpaper paste

Making scallops and wallpaper decoration

This project uses leftover pieces of wallpaper to create a border of scallops along the base of the cornice, and flower motifs around the window, to add to the decorative feel of the room. As well as involving little or no outlay, these ideas can be used to liven up a piece of furniture, or to make your own border or dado.

1 To create a scalloped border from wallpaper, place a dinner plate over the edge of a piece of wallpaper so that it is half on the paper. Mark the halfway point on each side of the plate with a strip of masking tape. Draw around the curved plate with a pencil. Continue to draw scalloped curves along the paper, always lining up the edge of the paper with the masking tape on the plate.

2 Place a cutting mat or piece of cardboard under the wallpaper to protect your work surface. Using a craft knife, carefully cut along the pencilled curves to create a row of scallops, ensuring that you do not cut through to the edge of the wallpaper. The scalloped border can now be pasted directly under the cornice.

3 Find two circular objects you can draw around; one should be larger than the other. Here we have used a saucer and a reel of masking tape. Draw around the saucer on lemon-checked wallpaper. This circle will form the basis of the flowerhead.

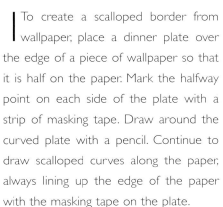

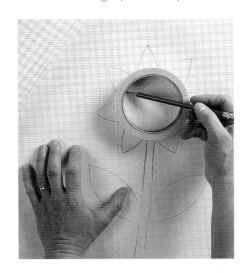

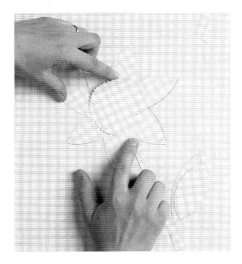

4 Draw a simple flower shape. The petals should extend no further than the original circle. Add a stalk and a pair of leaves. Then place the masking tape in the centre and draw around it. Place the tape on green-checked wallpaper. Draw round the inside of it.

5 Using pinking shears to create an appliquéd effect, cut out the centre section of the flower motif, and the rest of the flower motif from the lemon-checked wallpaper.

6 Using wallpaper paste, stick the flower design on to the wall, pressing it from the centre outwards to remove air bubbles. Cut smaller leaves from the green-checked paper and stick these on top of the yellow leaves. Repeat the process for further flower motifs.

MATERIALS

glassware

soft cloth

methylated spirits

masking tape

sponge

white emulsion paint

acrylic varnish

yellow acrylic paint

blue acrylic paint

stippling brush

fine pointed soft brush

acrylic spray varnish

Frosting glassware

Decorating glassware with this frosting technique is a quick and easy way to transform ordinary glass jugs or bowls into ornamental pieces for your home. Using little more than a tin of matt emulsion paint and some acrylic varnish, you will be able to frost your glassware to match your decor. Once you have tried the following few simple steps, you can go on to design your own exciting patterns.

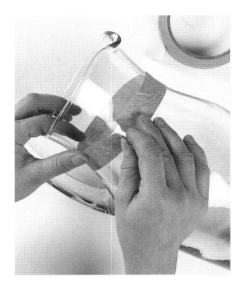

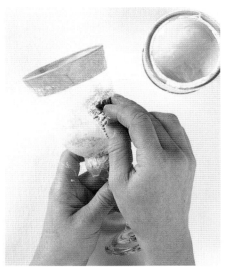

1 Wash the glass object thoroughly in hot soapy water, then rinse under the hot tap. Allow to dry completely and then wipe the whole surface with a clean soft cloth and methylated spirits to remove any remaining grease. Using masking tape, mask off any area that you wish to remain as clear glass.

2 Dip a small piece of sponge into white emulsion paint, then dab the sponge lightly all over the surface of the unmasked glass to achieve an even covering. Allow to dry completely.

3 Mix up a glaze using a small quantity of acrylic varnish and a blob of yellow acrylic paint. Then, using a stippling brush, jab the glaze over the top of the dry emulsion paint on the glass. Leave to dry completely.

4 Gently peel away the masking tape. Then sponge a white base coat over the clear glass and, when dry, stipple over a complementary colour glaze as shown in step 3. Alternatively, you can leave the glass clear.

5 Allow the paint to dry completely. Using a fine pointed soft brush, add further details over the top of the stippled paint in blue acrylic paint, covering the join of the two contrasting colours. Allow to dry, then spray the glass with clear varnish for protection.

MATERIALS

cushion pad

tape measure

fabric for cushion cover

tailor's chalk

dressmaking scissors or
pinking shears

fabric for piping and ties

piping cord

basting thread

pins

sewing machine

matching thread

iron

Making a cushion with ties

You can never have too many cushions, especially in a bedroom. These items of soft furnishing add a touch of softness and comfort to even the most austere of rooms, which in turn creates a relaxing environment. At the very least they can be used as excellent injury-free weapons in a child's room! This easy project features a practical square cushion made with decorative fabric ties. The use of two complementry fabrics – lime check and cobalt blue check – adds both a cheeky design quality and a sense of fun. If you prefer, you could use up odds and ends of fabric that may be lying about.

1 Measure the cushion pad. Allowing 2cm (¾in) extra all round, measure and mark up two squares of fabric using tailor's chalk, and a smaller piece 6cm (2⅜in) long and the same width as the squares for the flap. Cut out the pieces with dressmaking scissors. Then cut out contrasting fabric for the piping; this should be 4cm (1⅝in) wide and as long as the outer edge of the cover.

2 To make the piping, fold the contrasting strip in half lengthwise and place piping cord into the fold. Run a basting stitch through the fabric and cord to hold it in place. Then pin this around the edge of one of the fabric squares, raw edges matching, and machine stitch in position.

3 To make the cushion ties first cut out four pieces of contrasting fabric 20cm (8in) long and 10cm (4in) wide. Fold each piece lengthwise with right sides facing, then turn under the raw edges, and baste and machine stitch around the three sides. Turn the ties the right way out and press with a warm iron to neaten.

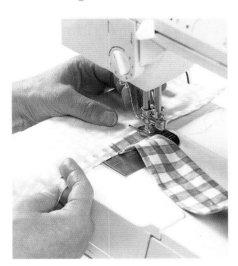

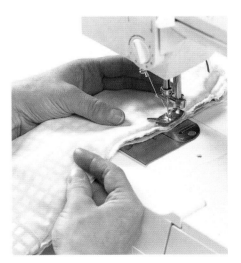

4 Turn under and stitch one edge of the unpiped fabric square. Place two ties on this edge. Baste, then machine stitch in place.

5 Match up the remaining ties on the edge of the piped fabric square; pin in place. Place the small flap of fabric over these ties against the edge of the square, right sides facing, enclosing the ties. Pin, baste and machine stitch the layers together to create an envelope-type flap.

6 Place the other fabric square on top of these layers, right sides together and the ties matching. Pin, baste and stitch around the remaining three sides of the cushion cover. Turn the cover the right side out through the flap. Insert the cushion pad and arrange the ties to finish.

MATERIALS

wooden frame

acrylic all-purpose primer

household paintbrush

fine-grade sandpaper

blue emulsion paint

masking tape

lime green emulsion paint

small paintbrush

turquoise paint

acrylic satin finish varnish

Painting a picture frame

If you have ever wasted precious time in a picture framing gallery trying to select the right frame for a much loved piece of art, then this is the project for you. It was only after years of disappointing results in choosing suitable frames that it became clear that the best results can be achieved by adapting and painting the frame yourself. In this way the frame can be coloured to enhance the image it frames and to co-ordinate with your chosen interior. In this project a plain wooden frame was adapted with the use of paint and masking tape to make a frame that not only relates well to the painting but also to its environment. Plain untreated wooden frames are often cheaper than gilt, lacquered or gesso ones, and they also offer you the opportunity to change the frame colour as often as you choose.

1 Brush a coat of acrylic all-purpose primer over the entire frame. This will seal the wood and cover any knots that may occur quite naturally in the wood of the frame. Allow to dry.

2 Rub the primed frame with fine-grade sandpaper to smooth the surface, then paint the frame with blue emulsion paint. To achieve a handpainted look, drag the paint on over the white primer, allowing some of the white primer to show through.

3 Allow the paint to dry. Then mask off the inner and outer edges of the frame with masking tape, leaving only the middle section visible.

4 Carefully apply lime green paint to the section of frame between the two masked edges. As before, drag the paint over the area, allowing the blue base coat to show through in fine lines. Allow the paint to dry.

5 Remove the masking tape carefully so as not to take the paint layer with it. If any paint is pulled off, touch up the area with a small dab of blue paint. Then rub the whole frame with fine-grade sandpaper. Using a small paintbrush, paint thin lines of turquoise paint on to the raised edges of the frame. Allow to dry, then seal the frame with a coat of acrylic satin finish varnish.

EXPERT TIPS

• *If you intend to paint a frame that you already have, remove the painting prior to priming. If this is not possible, protect the painting by covering it with paper and masking around the frame's inside edge.*

• *Try your hand at more adventurous paint effects on your frames, such as rag rolling or sponging. Often a combination of paint effects can work very well.*

49

MAKEOVER PROJECT

Moody Blues

The range of different blues used in this colour scheme create a slightly turbulent light, giving the room a moody, atmospheric quality. The addition of white in the colour scheme softens and freshens the overall feel.

Blue is a very popular colour for bedrooms; we may all like our beds to be warm but on the whole we like the actual room to be cool. With the invention of central heating, the use of blue in decorating schemes has increased. The inspiration for this room emerged from waking in the night to

PROJECTS FROM THIS
MAKEOVER SHOW YOU

- HOW TO PAINT
  ADJOINING SURFACES

- HOW TO PAINT A
  FLOOR

- HOW TO MAKE A
  PADDED PICTURE
  FRAME

- HOW TO DECORATE
  CERAMICS

catch the last of the rolling thunder, when flashes of electric blue light streaked into the room. There is the most amazing sense of calm after a storm. This makeover is an attempt to regain that feeling of exhilaration.

As blue is a receding colour, seeming to create space, you can apply the paint flat without the fear of reflective intensity. In this room the walls and ceiling were painted a warm mid-blue, the window and door a deep cobalt blue, and the woodwork a mid-lavender blue. The cornice was painted slightly unevenly in a pale lilac blue, while the floor was given a distressed finish using a cool sea-blue.

PREPARATION

Stick down any loose wallpaper with wallpaper paste, and fill any cracks in the plaster with filler. As the room will be painted with matt emulsion paint, pay particular attention to the condition of the walls. Make sure that they are thoroughly rubbed down and smoothed prior to painting, otherwise imperfections will show up clearly. When painting with different blues, ensure that the colours do not overlap; careful masking is essential.

Choose your accessories for the bedroom carefully. In this room, white was used together with punchy checked fabrics which are widely available in high street stores. They add a warming sense of welcome to what could be an austere environment.

PAINTING ADJOINING SURFACES

When painting a cornice in a different colour to the ceiling and walls, it is essential to mask off the surfaces on either side of it. This will ensure that paint does not spatter on the ceiling or wall, and that the painted edges of the cornice are straight and even. Choose a colour of paint that works well with the adjoining surfaces to avoid clashing. Here, the cornice is painted in pale lilac blue while the adjoining walls are painted in mid blue.

1 Stick lengths of low-tack masking tape along the edges of the ceiling and wall adjoining the cornice.

2 Using a household brush, paint the cornice with pale lilac blue emulsion paint, ensuring that the brushstrokes are confined within the lengths of masking tape to produce a clean straight edge. Allow the paint to dry thoroughly.

3 Remove the masking tape and re-apply it on the painted cornice, butting it up to the edge of the wall. Then apply the mid-blue emulsion on the wall right up to the cornice to produce a clean straight edge with no overlapping of colour.

Painting a floor

MATERIALS

hammer

coarse-grade sandpaper

acrylic all-purpose primer

household brushes

emulsion paint: pink, sea-blue, creamy yellow

large soft brush

floor varnish

Floor painting can be the ideal answer to matching up a variety of paint colours in a room. It also lends itself to a wide and varied choice of application. There is a huge range of commercial colours available; alternatively, colours can be hand-mixed with limitless possibilities. Colours can be laid on top of one another to build up different decorative effects. Any number of designs can be used to enhance or contrast with your already existing colour theme. A new floor can be antiqued or an old one brought up to date. With the use of contemporary floor varnishes widely available, there is no reason why your painted floor should not last forever.

1 Inspect the floorboards before you begin and hammer down any prominent nail heads. Then rub the floor vigorously with coarse-grade sandpaper wrapped around a block of wood to create a smooth surface. Pay particular attention to boards which are warped or split. Paint the floor with acrylic all-purpose primer and allow to dry.

2 Using a household brush, apply a base coat of pink emulsion paint over the floorboards, dragging the brush over the surface to produce long brush-strokes. Allow to dry.

3 Dip a large soft brush into sea-blue emulsion paint, then drag it over the base coat, allowing some of the pink to show through. Leave to dry.

4 Using a smaller household brush, apply creamy yellow emulsion paint sporadically along the floorboards, carefully following the line of the grain and the previous brushmarks.

5 When the paint is thoroughly dry, apply two coats of hardwearing floor varnish to seal and protect the aged and distressed floor. Allow the first coat to dry before applying the second. Leave the varnish to dry completely before walking on the floor.

MATERIALS

image

ruler

pencil

thin card

scissors

strong card

fabric

tailor's chalk

dressmaking scissors,
optional

craft knife

interfacing

fabric glue

double-sided tape

perspex

sticky tape

Making a padded frame

Almost everyone has a favourite picture or photograph yet it can be difficult finding the right frame to display it. As a result, the picture may be left propped between objects on a shelf, collecting dust and gradually becoming more dog-eared and scratched. This project solves the problem by showing you how to make your own picture or photo frame which can be covered in a fabric of your choice to match your decorative colour scheme. This will add a homely touch to any image and, whether it stands alone or as part of a collection, it will definitely enhance your bedroom.

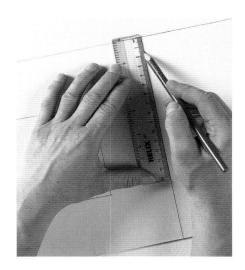

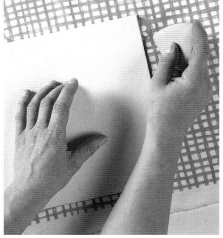

1 Measure the image. Draw a square on thin card slightly larger than the image. Then draw a square around this one 3cm (1¼in) larger all round than the inner square. Draw two more squares the same size as the outer square. Cut out the three large squares. Cut a wedge-shaped frame support from strong card.

2 Place one card square on to your chosen fabric. Allowing for a 2cm (¾in) turnover, mark the fabric all around the square with tailor's chalk. Repeat to mark a second square. Cut out the fabric squares using dressmaking scissors. Then cut out enough fabric to cover the card frame support.

3 Cut out the square window from the first card square. Cut two pieces of interfacing and glue these to the card frame. Glue one fabric square over the padding, wrapping the edges over the back. Cut a diagonal cross in the fabric over the window. Glue the fabric triangles to the back of the card.

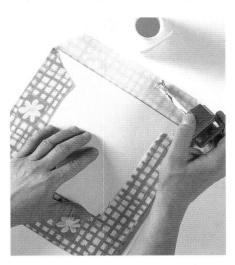

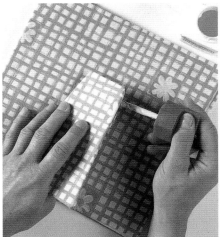

4 Lay the remaining fabric square face down and place a second card square on top. Stick the fabric on to the card, folding and sticking the edges down securely. Then apply glue over the side of the card with the fabric overlap and place the remaining card square on top. Attach the image to the centre of this card square with double-sided tape.

5 Stick a piece of perspex to the inside of the window using sticky tape. Glue the card surrounding the image and press the fabric-covered window frame on top of this, with the padded side uppermost. Stick fabric to the frame support with fabric glue, then glue the frame support to the back of the frame with the aid of a small cardboard hinge.

EXPERT TIPS

• *Choose fabric appropriate to the scale of the frame, as a large-patterned fabric will be lost on a small-sized frame.*

• *Use fast-drying fabric glue and wash your hands between each step to avoid ruining the fabric of the frame.*

Painting ceramics

ceramics

masking tape

artist's brush

ceramic paint

low-tack tape

solvent

cotton bud

paper dots

stippling brush

When you change the colour scheme of your bedroom, and go to the trouble of finding new fabrics and lighting, it is often not possible to re-use existing accessories because they just do not match the new scheme. This project gives you a chance to redesign or change, in as dramatic a way as you like, any of those favourite jugs, bowls, cups and saucers that do not fit in with your decor. Painting ceramics is both inexpensive and satisfying to do as it recycles old ceramics as well as providing an excuse to vent your artistic skills, however limited they might be. In these examples artistic flair is quite unnecessary, as using masking tape makes it easy to add decorative stripes and checks to transform plain ceramics instantly.

1 Wash the ceramic piece and make sure that your hands are clean and free of grease; any grease on the ceramic piece will result in the paint being repelled. Dry the ceramic piece thoroughly. For a checked design, stick lengths of masking tape in vertical stripes around the side of your ceramic piece, leaving a gap of approximately 12mm (½in) between each length.

2 Using a pointed artist's brush, apply mid-blue ceramic paint over the unmasked areas. Allow to dry, then peel off the masking tape. Remask the ceramic piece with horizontal bands (this time low-tack tape), again leaving 12mm (½in) between each band. Paint darker blue ceramic paint over the unmasked areas. Clean off any over-spills of paint with solvent and a cotton bud.

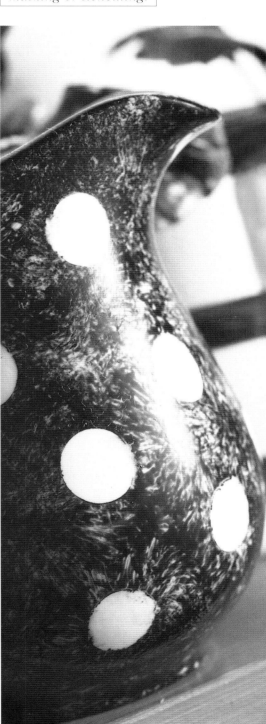

3 Allow the paint to dry, then peel off the masking tape carefully. If any paint pulls off, apply a few dabs of paint over the top to repair the damage.

4 To create a spotted design, place paper dots randomly over the piece. Stipple ceramic paint on to the surface to cover it completely. Leave to dry, then carefully peel off the paper dots to reveal clean white ceramic spots underneath. Clean off any unwanted glaze using a cotton bud. If desired, you can paint in the white dots with a contrasting colour.

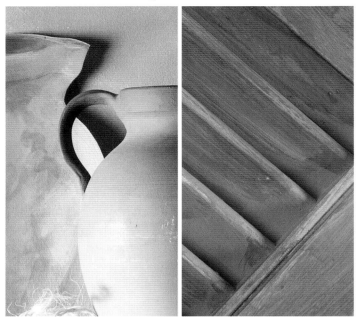

MAKEOVER PROJECT

Rich Terracotta

Terracotta evokes sunlight and heat, and the rich terracotta walls in this colour scheme create a warm, cosy atmosphere, ideal for a bedroom. The blue floorboards complement the walls, and soften the effect of the terracotta.

Terracotta is a very popular colour, perhaps because it evokes those exotic warm countries where terracotta is so often used and where you can see and appreciate the wonderful effect and depth that the use of this rich warm colour can offer. Collect a few old terracotta pots together and

PROJECTS FROM THIS
MAKEOVER SHOW YOU

- HOW TO DRY-BRUSH
  AND AGE SURFACES

- HOW TO MAKE A
  DÉCOUPAGED *TROMPE-
  L'OEIL* JUG

- HOW TO ANTIQUE
  WOODEN SHUTTERS

examine their colours; you will see that terracotta is actually composed of a range of brownish-orange colours. Use a few colours and blend them together.

As the walls were the dominant part of this room, they were decorated with a terracotta colourwash. A colourwash imitates the appearance of old-fashioned, distemper-painted walls, and this paint effect gives the room a sunny, bleached atmosphere, exactly what was wanted in this texture-rich natural interior. Colourwashing is an easy technique to do and quite a useful technique if the wall surface is at all lumpy or irregular.

PREPARATION

When colourwashing, lots of liquid may be splashed around the room, so make sure that any furnishings that cannot be removed are covered with both dust sheets and polythene to protect them from staining. Also ensure that any electrical outlets, such as sockets, are switched off, the plugs removed, and the outlets covered in polythene and sealed with masking tape.

If the walls are in good decorative order and are already either painted white or another suitable tone, then all that is required is to give the walls a good wash with a sponge and a bowl of warm water. This should remove any dirt and dust. If there are any greasy patches, remove them with a general household cleaner prior to colourwashing.

If the walls are a dark colour, they will require priming prior to being colourwashed. If drips and runs occur when priming, and these cannot be blended in using a clean damp brush, allow the area to dry completely then re-prime, taking care to blend the primer at the edges. This should help disguise the area and diffuse any darker patches.

DRY-BRUSHING AND AGEING

These techniques are easy to do following the steps below. They are also useful when decorating woodwork as they add depth and texture to what would otherwise be areas of flat colour.

1 Mask off the wall and floor on either side of the surface to be painted. Mix a wash using 1 part pale grey emulsion and 3 parts acrylic varnish, then add a little water until the mixture is like milk. Apply a base coat of the pale grey wash.

2 Allow the base coat to dry. Then dip a dry brush into deeper grey emulsion and drag this over the base coat, allowing streaks of the pale grey to show through. Leave to dry.

3 Mix ageing glaze by adding a small amount of burnt umber pigment to acrylic varnish. Add more pigment as required to achieve the desired depth of tone. Brush the ageing glaze over the painted surface and leave to dry.

Découpaged jug

MATERIALS

paper

acrylic all-purpose primer

household brush

pencil

cutting mat or cardboard

craft knife

emulsion paint: terracotta, brown, green

acrylic varnish

artist's brushes

varnish brush

Découpage is the cutting out and sticking down of paper decoration, and it is a good alternative to stencilling. This project shows how to make a paper terracotta jug to use as a *trompe-l'oeil* decoration on a bedroom wall. You can either stick or simply lean your flat jug against the wall to create a piece of decorative fun.

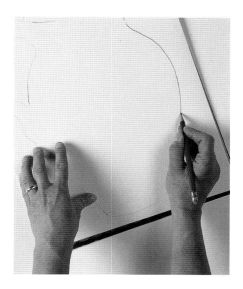

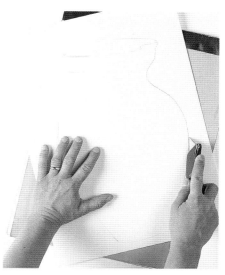

EXPERT TIPS

• *If you don't want to paint a decoration for your wall, cut out an image from a book or magazine. Glue this to a piece of card, trim around the edges, then varnish over the top and use as shown.*

• *Create your own family portrait by photocopying photos. Brush with ageing glaze to create a sepia tone, then stick on to the wall. Hang a silver-sprayed card frame over the image.*

1 Paint a piece of paper with acrylic all-purpose primer; paper will discolour if left unprotected, so a coat of primer will not only help to prevent damage but will also make a good surface to work on. Then, using a pencil, draw or trace the outline of your image on to the paper.

2 Place the paper on a cutting mat or piece of cardboard to protect the underlying work surface. Then, using a craft knife, carefully cut out the pencilled shape, working slowly and turning the paper as you go to retain the soft curves of the design.

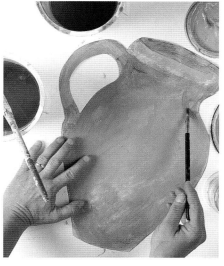

3 Mix up a dilute wash of 1 part terracotta emulsion paint to 3 parts acrylic varnish. When mixed thoroughly, add a little water until the mixture is the consistency of milk. Using an artist's brush, paint the cut-out jug with the terracotta wash to establish a three-dimensional effect.

4 Using a finer artist's brush, add patches of brown and green emulsion paint to shade the sides of the jug, highlight the rim and emphasize the jug's curved shape. Keep stepping back from the image to judge the effect, correcting any details as necessary as you are painting.

5 Allow the paint to dry, then apply a coat of acrylic varnish over the top to protect the image. Allow the découpaged jug to dry flat.

Antiquing wooden shutters

MATERIALS

wooden shutters

fine-grade sandpaper

cloth

household paintbrush

terracotta vinyl silk paint

coarse-grade sandpaper

fine artist's brush

dark brown emulsion paint

burnt umber acrylic paint

satin finish acrylic varnish

Aged and antiqued wooden shutters immediately create a look that is reminiscent of foreign holidays and exciting times. When used in a room like this, they add a distinct air of authenticity. Sometimes shutters are preferable for a window for practical reasons, for instance in a bathroom with a large sash window to the front, where partial privacy is required. Shutters can offer the same privacy, warmth and light control as other more traditional forms of window dressing, but at the same time they create a more unusual or architectural finish. Antiquing shutters is a simple and effective way of linking a decorating theme such as the Mediterranean, sunsoaked feel of this room. The following step-by-step guide shows you how to set about antiquing a pair of shutters.

1 Rub the shutters lightly with fine-grade sandpaper, then wipe them over with a damp cloth to remove any dust. Using a household paintbrush, apply a coat of terracotta vinyl silk paint over each shutter, taking care to catch any drips or runs. Check that as the paint is applied to one side of the louvres that no paint is pooling on the other side.

2 When the paint is completely dry – usually two hours or so – rub the shutters vigorously with coarse-grade sandpaper, turning the shutters as you work to give an even feel. Then rub the edges of the shutter frame with sandpaper to remove sections of paint completely; this will create an impression of natural wear and tear.

3 With a fine artist's brush, apply patches of dark brown emulsion paint to the heavily sanded areas and rub this in with your finger. This will create the effect of old wood under the terracotta paintwork. Then continue to sand and scrape at the paint until a satisfactory look is achieved.

4 Mix up some ageing glaze by adding a blob of burnt umber acrylic paint to a tin of satin finish acrylic varnish and mixing thoroughly. Apply this in sweeping brushstrokes across the louvres and around the frame in an anti-clockwise direction. Allow to dry, then apply a coat of clear varnish for protection.

MAKEOVER PROJECT

Neutral Tones

The muted tones of cream, vanilla and pale sultry grey featured in this decorating scheme, balanced with the simplicity and understatement of the furnishings, have created an effect of elegance and sophistication. This is a bedroom to lounge around in wearing sheer silk pyjamas, should you have the inclination.

The inspiration for this room evolved from many sources: old French novels and films, antique cotton lace sheets, a small ceramic cherub rescued from a flea market, and a soft white rose

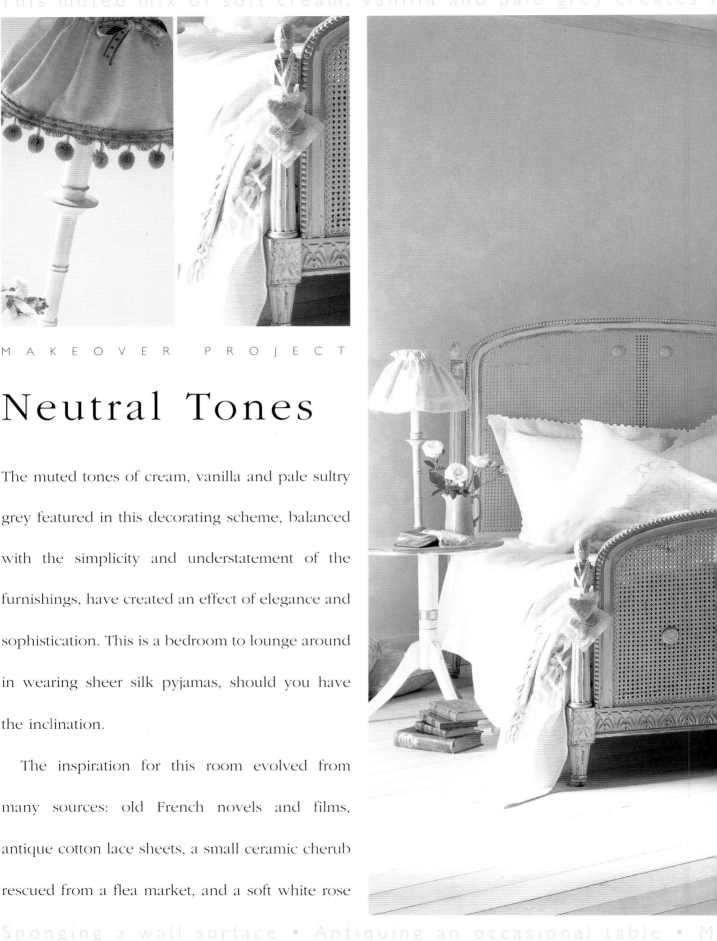

PROJECTS FROM THIS
MAKEOVER SHOW YOU

- HOW TO SPONGE A
  WALL

- HOW TO ANTIQUE A
  TABLE

- HOW TO MAKE A FABRIC
  LAMPSHADE

- HOW TO SEW LAVENDER
  SACHETS

still glistening with dew. When these objects were collected together, a paint colour card was consulted and the choice of soft shades of vanilla, lily white, cream and pale grey emerged. It also became obvious that part of the attraction of these inspirational objects was their time-worn appearance, and so it was important that this was also reflected in the room, to create the impression of faded elegance.

The paint was applied using differing techniques, thus avoiding any hard edges or defining lines. Subtle tones of colour were used and no aspect of the room was overstated. The effect is a soft blending of colours.

PREPARATION

Before you begin to paint, go over the ceiling, walls and woodwork to check for peeling paper, air bubbles and any cracks. Stick any loose paper back in position with wallpaper paste. Cut any air bubbles and stick back in position with paste. This is especially important for ceilings; if loose paper is painted over, the weight of the wet paint might cause it to tear and fall, and bring with it a section of ceiling plaster. Fill in any cracks with all-purpose filler, allow to dry, then sand to a smooth finish. This preparation is essential to ensure a smooth finish.

Prepare your paint colours in readiness for using them. The use of neutral colours has always been popular; pale tones can be a sound starting point for adding extra colour, which can be gently added at any stage.

SPONGING A WALL

Before sponging a wall, you must first prime it with acrylic all-purpose primer. This seals the surface and provides a good surface on which to apply glaze. If the surface is not sealed, the glaze will soak into the wall and spoil the effect. In this makeover of neutral tones, the walls and ceiling were delicately sponged in a pale vanilla and acrylic glaze over a white primed surface.

EXPERT TIP

● *When using acrylic varnish, allow yourself enough time and material to be able to cover whole sections. If the telephone rings when you are halfway across the wall, leave it to ring. If you stop a paint effect in full flow, you will return to a distinctive line. This will become worse when you begin again and retrace your steps, making the line even deeper in tone.*

1 Using a household brush, paint the wall surface with acrylic all-purpose primer. Apply the primer in all directions, up and down, side to side and diagonally so that brushmarks are not visible. Ensure the coverage is even. Allow to dry.

2 In a pot, mix together 1 part pale vanilla emulsion paint with 2 parts acrylic varnish. Use a paintbrush to stir the mixture together well; this is the sponging glaze.

3 Dip a sponge lightly into the vanilla glaze, then dab the sponge on the wall to create a pattern of small dots. Continue to dab the sponge over the surface, dipping it into the glaze as needed, until the entire wall is covered in a soft, mottled paint effect.

MATERIALS

wooden table

sandpaper

acrylic all-purpose
primer

household brush

white emulsion paint

burnt umber pigment

acrylic varnish

gold paint

Antiquing a table

The effect of antiquing produces and imitates the effects of time on paint and adds a worn look to the newest of pieces, allowing for a mellow blend between genuinely old and new. This small pine occasional table was transformed into a delightful piece which, when intermingled with other genuine antiques in the room, adds a degree of elegance and charm. It also has the added advantage of being user-friendly and, because of the acrylic varnish, knock-resistant.

1 Rub the table with sandpaper wrapped around a block to smooth the surface and give it a key to enable the paint to adhere. Then prime it with acrylic all-purpose primer to seal the surface, ensuring that the table is evenly covered. Allow to dry.

2 When the primer is thoroughly dry, rub the table lightly with sandpaper so that small patches of the original surface show through the primer.

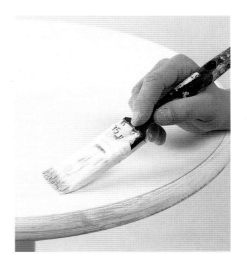

3 Using a household brush, apply a coat of white emulsion paint thinly and evenly over the entire table. Leave to dry, then sand the surface very lightly again for a smooth finish.

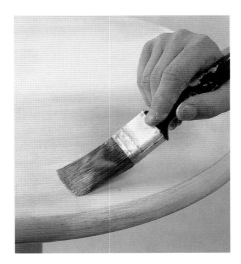

4 Mix the ageing glaze by adding a small amount of burnt umber pigment to acrylic varnish. Add more pigment as required to achieve the desired depth of tone. Brush the glaze over the surface of the table and leave to dry completely.

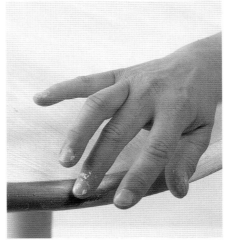

5 Dip a finger in gold paint and rub it roughly around the edge of the tabletop to imitate gilt edging. Add a further gold band around the table leg if desired. The intermittent application of the gold emulates the natural wear on the edge of the table. The end result might not fool an antiques expert but it will look authentic in a room scheme such as this.

EXPERT TIPS

• *For an authentic look, make sure that the table is completely sealed with several coats of acrylic varnish, sanding with fine-grade sandpaper between each coat.*

• *If the table is to receive heavy use, cut a glass or perspex top to protect the table surface.*

Making a fabric lampshade

MATERIALS

lampshade frame

tape measure

fabric

dressmaking scissors

iron

pins

sewing thread

sewing machine

tailor's chalk

pom-pom fringing

craft knife

tapestry needle or
safety pin

ribbon or cord

Lighting can significantly change the ambience of any room. In this room a soft natural glow was required and this was achieved by the use of a handmade lampshade which offered both a delicate elegance and a gentle muted illumination. The basic shade can be enhanced by the use of a decorative fringe or ribbon, which can be sewn on to the edge of the skirt of the lampshade. The fabric chosen in this project was a pale fine-weave flame-retardant linen; it was gently gathered around the top of a lampshade frame and then pulled together with ribbon and allowed to hang in soft folds over the lamp base. Fringing completed the look. This lampshade is easy to make and will add a charming personal touch to any bedroom.

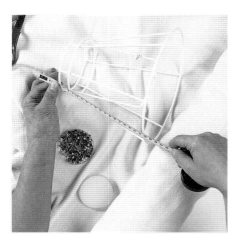

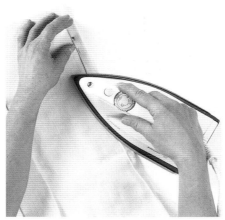

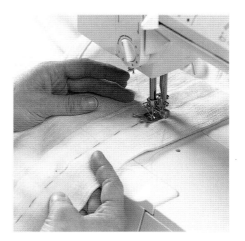

1 To calculate the amount of fabric needed for the lampshade, measure the circumference of the frame at the widest point then multiply this by two; this will give the width of fabric required. To calculate the length needed, measure the height of the lampshade frame. Then add 12cm (4¾in) to this to allow for turning and hemming at top and bottom.

2 Cut out the fabric with dressmaking scissors. Carefully fold over 2cm (¾in) of one long edge of the fabric and press with an iron. Then fold the edge over 6cm (2⅜in) and press again. Insert pins to secure the fold. Repeat this process at the opposite long edge of the fabric, but this time making the second fold only 2cm (¾in) deep.

3 Baste the two hems then, using a sewing machine, stitch the hems 3mm (⅛in) from each inner edge. On the wider folded edge, measure 2cm (¾in) from the line of hem stitches and mark this along the whole width of fabric using tailor's chalk. Baste along this chalked line and then machine stitch, finishing the threads off properly at each end.

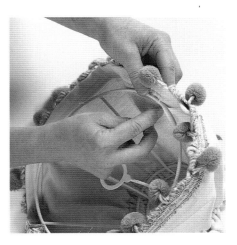

4 Lay the fabric flat so the hems are facing downwards. Cut a length of pom-pom fringing to fit along the length of the lampshade. Pin this along the hemmed edge of the lampshade. Then baste and machine stitch the fringe in place along the line of hem stitches.

5 Fold the fabric in half, right sides facing, and raw edges together. Leaving a 12mm (½in) seam, stitch the sides together. Turn the shade right side out. Cut a slit in between the two lines of stitching in the top layer of fabric at the top of the shade. Using a tapestry needle, thread ribbon through the slit and along the channel, gathering the fabric as you go. Tie the ribbon ends.

6 Fit the lampshade frame inside the fabric shade and secure in position with large loop stitches sewn around the gathered fabric and the top wire ring of the frame. Then lift the shade and give it a gentle shake to settle the fabric in place. Stitch small looping stitches attaching the folds of fabric to the bottom ring of the frame. Attach the lampshade to the lamp base to finish.

Lavender sachets

muslin

dressmaking scissors

sewing thread

sewing machine

dried lavender

paper

iron

pins

ribbon

button or bow

Lavender scent always conjures up images of long carefree summer holidays spent in the south of France where the days are trouble free and the nights warm and romantic. Aromatherapists and herbalists recognize the beneficial qualities that lavender has to offer when used as an essential oil; it is in fact a natural sedative and has been used since time began to calm and soothe our nerves. The scent that it gives off evokes feelings of relaxation and peace, making it a perfect companion to a good night's sleep. This project shows how to create your own lavender sachets which you can hang on bed posts, mirror frames or drawer handles in the bedroom to fill the room with the soft perfume of lavender.

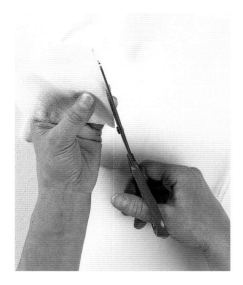

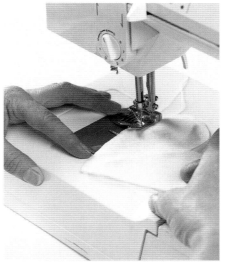

1 Sachets are usually square, circular or heart-shaped. Carefully cut two matching shapes from a piece of muslin for each sachet. Here, two heart shapes are cut out.

2 Baste the two shapes together, then machine stitch around the shapes, about 6mm (¼in) from the edge, leaving the last few centimetres unsewn. Gently turn the sachet the right way out through the unstitched gap, teasing the fabric into the correct shape.

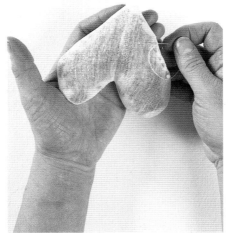

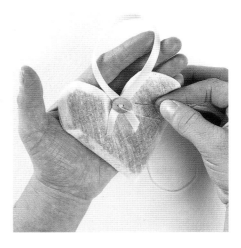

3 Fill the muslin sachet with dried lavender. To do this, make a small paper funnel, place the end of the funnel into the muslin pocket, then fill it with dried lavender and gently shake in the contents. Don't over-fill the sachet as extra space allows the full fragrance of the lavender to be released.

4 Turn in the edges of the opening in the sachet and press gently with a hot iron. Pin, then baste the opening closed. Pressing the edges together, carefully sew the remaining edge by hand using small neat slipstitches. Then gently pull the heart sachet back into shape and shake it to disperse the contents evenly.

5 Attach a loop of ribbon to the centre of the sachet with a few small stitches. Then stitch a button or bow on to the point where the ribbon is joined to the sachet; this will disguise any clumsy stitching and adds a dainty finishing touch.

MAKEOVER PROJECT

Matisse Style

With its decor of pink, green, turquoise and yellow, this bedroom emits a sunny, happy atmosphere. An eclectic mix of colourful fabrics, ornaments and flowering plants adds to the character in the room.

The inspiration for this room came from a painting entitled 'The Open Window' by Henri Matisse, which is actually featured in the room, hanging above the bed. The effect of the painting is of a riot of colour and pattern, and quite bohemian in feel.

PROJECTS FROM THIS
MAKEOVER SHOW YOU

- HOW TO BLEND
  COLOURS

- HOW TO PAINT A FRIEZE

- HOW TO STENCIL
  FABRIC

- HOW TO MAKE A
  CURTAINED SCREEN

In this makeover, a similar effect of colour and space was sought. So, the walls were painted in turquoise and pink, with the wall texture built up by the use of several tones of colour, applied using brushes of various sizes. The wooden floor was also distressed in a bright blue, while the window frame and door were painted in a rich bright yellow, with orange dragged over the top. The furniture was distressed with turquoise over a sea-green base; the wrought iron chair was chosen because it echoed the iron railings in the picture. The use of several colours is effective because the colours are all of the same tonal value.

PREPARATION

It may appear at first glance that the need for careful preparation for a room like this is unnecessary, as the finished look is quite rough. Nevertheless, the usual rules of decorating still apply; the walls and ceiling still need to be checked over and any cracks filled with all-purpose filler. The look was achieved by layering the paint, so the need for good adherent surfaces is paramount. To achieve this, rub down thoroughly all painted surfaces and prime them securely with acrylic all-purpose primer. Mask off areas of different colour before applying paint so that you get clean straight edges.

Choose the paint colours that you intend to use in your bedroom and, if you are unsure, paint a small test area on a bedroom wall to check that the colours work well together before starting.

BLENDING COLOURS

Although the colour of the wall surrounding the window may look pink, it is actually a combination of three different paint colours, which have been blended together using different sizes of brush. This method of blending colour gives greater depth and interest to a surface and can be a useful way of lightening a dark area of wall without there being too much contrast. It is also useful if the walls to be painted are slightly chipped or pitted, as the nature of the paint effect is to produce an aged, distressed look.

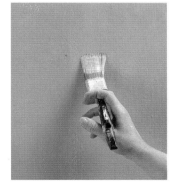

1 Using a household brush, apply a coat of medium-pink emulsion paint over the surface. Brush it up and down to cover the surface evenly.

2 Using a smaller brush, apply pale orange emulsion paint over the pink, blending it carefully into the first coat. Using a smaller brush changes the scale of brushmark and the tone of colour, which adds to the overall effect.

3 Using a large household brush, apply pale pink emulsion, blending the colour roughly into the first two coats. The finished effect should be a mixture of the three different paint colours, while still allowing patches of each colour to show.

Painting a frieze

MATERIALS

ruler

soft pencil

spirit level

artist's brush

emulsion paint: white,
orange, red, green

varnish brush

clear acrylic varnish

Paint can be used to create a huge range of visual effects. Even if you have never painted before, it is possible to paint a frieze on your wall. If your artistic skills are limited, you can copy an image from a book or magazine or, as here, from part of the Matisse painting. In this project, a shelf was placed beneath the image for an amusing touch. If you feel unhappy at the thought of copying freehand, there are processes you can use to translate your chosen image from book to wall. The first thing to do is to trace over the image using a pencil. Then draw a grid over the top. Next, number all the squares, and draw a grid directly on to the wall to the size you intend to have your image. Number these squares so that they correspond to your original grid, then transfer your image square by square. Alternatively, if you have access to a slide projector, you can project and enlarge your image directly on to the wall.

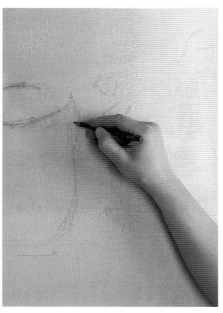

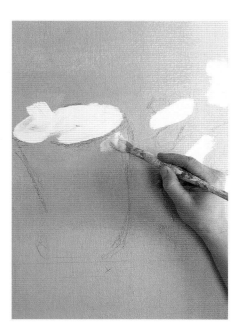

1 Measure and mark the area of the wall where you intend to paint your image. Use a spirit level to ensure that the marked line is straight. This will act as a guide when painting.

2 Using a soft pencil, begin to sketch in the outlines of your chosen motif on to the wall. This particular image consisted of three pots of colourful flowering geraniums.

3 Starting with the lightest tones, begin to apply patches of emulsion paint over the pencilled outlines. Do not paint neat brushstrokes; be bold and daub the paint on the wall. Aim for a random effect.

4 Add touches of orange and red paint to the frieze, applying it roughly to build up the design. The brushstrokes should simply suggest the flowers, rather than be accurate reproductions of actual petals.

5 Add daubs of green paint to suggest the leaves to complete your painted image. Allow to dry thoroughly, then brush a coat of clear varnish over the top to seal the frieze and protect it from any abrasions.

Stencilling fabric

The work of the artist Matisse has long influenced fabric and wallpaper designers. The wonderful use of colour and design within Matisse's paintings positively oozes enthusiasm. In this project, you can learn how to print fabric with bright cheerful colours – orange, yellow, red, cobalt blue and brilliant emerald green – to create your own bit of the south of France. This Matisse-inspired fabric can then be used as curtaining, as a bed cover, as a dressing table skirt, or made into cushions to brighten up any bedroom.

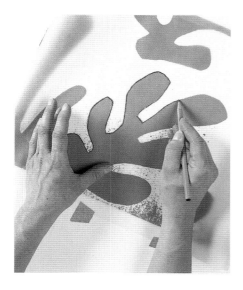

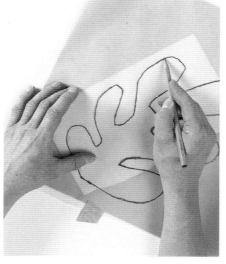

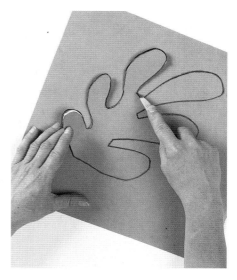

1 Photocopy two or three images from some of Matisse's paintings, enlarging them if desired. The shapes here were taken from two works: 'The Sheaf' (1953), and 'The Parakeet and the Mermaid' (1952). Trace around the photocopied images.

2 Place the carbon paper on top of the stencil card, and lay the tracing on top. Secure with masking tape. Go over the outlines with pencil to transfer the image. Then remove the tracing and carbon paper and go over the outlines on the stencil card with a thick black waterproof marker pen.

3 Place the stencil card on a cutting mat to protect the work surface. Then, using a sharp craft knife, carefully cut around the outside edge of the black line. Try to cut as smoothly as possible as ragged edges will not give a distinctive shape to the stencil. Discard the cut-out piece of card.

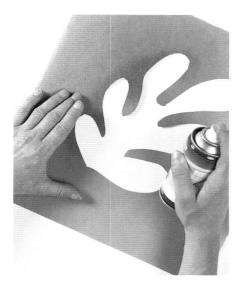

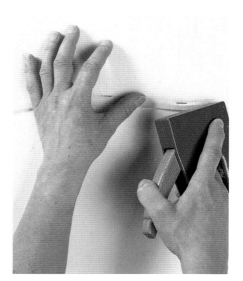

4 Spray the stencil with waterproof varnish, allow to dry then turn the stencil over and repeat. This will make the stencil stronger and will stop it becoming soggy with the fabric paint.

5 Pour a small quantity of the two colours that you wish to mix into a resealable container (as you may need to store the colour) and mix with a clean brush until integrated. Use the mixed colour immediately; if the mix is left to stand, stir again just before using.

6 Stretch the fabric to be printed. This can be done easily over a pasting table. First, cover the pasting table with an old roll of lining paper. Then lay the fabric on top and staple the edges along both ends and a couple of times down the length, ensuring that it is taut.

EXPERT TIP
● *If this is your first attempt at stencilling fabric do not be too ambitious in your choice of image – the simpler the better. It is easier to work with a limited colour palette as it enables you to work more quickly and there is less risk of mistakes.*

7 Using a tape measure and a soft pencil, measure and mark out on the fabric where you want your printed shapes to go. If you are intending to devise a repeating pattern, after marking where your shapes will go, you need to decide on which colour goes where. Lightly mark each square with the initials of the chosen colour to prevent any confusion when the printing starts.

8 Place the stencil centrally over the designated square. Secure it on to the fabric with four small tabs of low-tack masking tape in the corners. Dip a stippling brush lightly into a pot of fabric paint and, starting in the middle of the stencil, stipple paint over the fabric, working slowly out to the edges. Do not overload the brush or paint will drip on to the fabric.

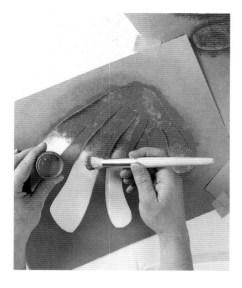

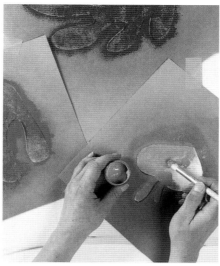

• Make sure that the fabric that you are printing on has the right absorbency for the fabric paint you intend to use. This can be tested by applying the paint to an off-cut of the fabric and seeing the results. Usually a natural fibre fabric will be more receptive to fabric paint.

• Consider where you will use your newly stencilled fabric. If you want the fabric to be washable, you will need to use washproof paint. Always read the labels of fabric paint carefully.

9 Repeat the same process with the second stencil, using a different colour. Make sure you do not lean on the first painted stencil as you work, in case you smudge the paint.

10 Move on to the third stencil and stipple a third colour of paint on to the fabric in the same way as in step 8. Carefully remove the stencils to reveal the stencilled images.

11 Measure the pattern with a tape measure, taking note of the distances between the various shapes. In this way you will be able to repeat the same layout along the fabric to make a repeating pattern.

12 Continue to stencil the fabric until it is covered. Then remove the stencils and allow the paint to dry. If there are any areas where the paint has leaked under the edges of the stencil, use a small soft pointed brush to paint over these, enlarging the shapes where necessary. If you wish to add any freehand detail to your painted fabric it can be done at this point.

Making a curtained screen

A screen is a useful and practical accessory in a bedroom. It can be used to section off areas of a room discreetly, for instance to create a dressing area, or it can be used as a practical object on which to hang clothes. Alternatively, a screen can simply be an attractive item of furniture which adds a flamboyant touch to a room. Inspired by the way in which the screen in the Matisse room enabled several fabrics to be displayed, softening the room with both colour and texture, this project takes a rather plain open screen, and transforms it into a wonderfully ornamental piece of furniture. Screen frames are available in varying forms, ranging from flat-packed kits to those already assembled. For the purposes of this project it is assumed that the screen frame has already been assembled.

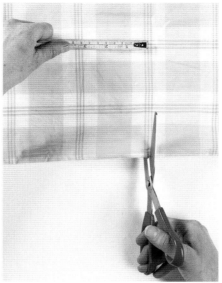

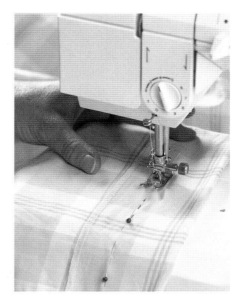

1 Using a household paintbrush, paint the screen frame in your desired colour of emulsion paint. Brush on the initial coat thinly as this will act as both a priming agent and a sealant. Allow to dry, then rub the frame down with fine-grade sandpaper. Apply a second coat.

2 Measure the height and width of each panel of the screen, adding 4cm (1½in) to each measurement to allow for hems. Cut out your chosen fabric accordingly. Turn over each long side of the fabric 12mm (½in) and press, then machine stitch.

3 Fold over 12mm (½in) of the fabric at the short edges and press. Turn over a further 3cm (1¼in), baste and machine stitch. Pin and baste another line 12mm (½in) from the hem line and parallel to it on both top and bottom hems, then machine stitch along this line.

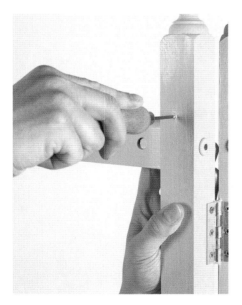

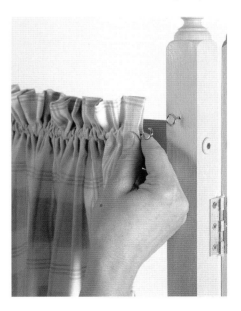

4 Using a bradawl, make a small hole in the four corners of each of the screen panels. Screw a small screw eye into each hole. Cut lengths of curtain wire to fit between each pair of hooks.

5 Screw a small hanging hook into one end of a cut piece of curtain wire. Feed it through the stitched channel at the top of each curtain. Repeat to thread the bottom channel. Screw on a hook to the opposite end of each wire.

6 Attach each of the curtains to the screen panels by hooking the hanging hooks through the screw eyes at the top and bottom of each panel of the frame. Readjust the curtain gathers as necessary for an even finish.

Brushes

BADGER SOFTENER

A necessary expense for any serious decorative artist, this brush is made from very soft, long bristles of pure badger hair. Use it to tickle away brushstrokes from wet glazes and to give an out-of-focus appearance. It is essential for marbling work and useful in creating a colourwashed effect. Meticulous cleaning is important as badger brushes are expensive to replace. Condition them with hair conditioner regularly.

FLOGGER

This brush has extremely long, floppy bristles which, when gently tapped into wet glaze, create the distinctive flecks seen in natural wood-grains such as oak.

ARTIST'S FITCHES

Usually made from hog's hair and quite stiff, fitches are invaluable as detailing brushes and for mixing smaller quantities of paint. Cheap fitches are fine, unless you are using them for mural work in which case better quality brushes will give a more even brushstroke. The bristles of good-quality fitches are slightly curved in towards the top of the brush, rather than being unnaturally straight.

FINE ARTIST'S BRUSHES

For detailing and fine mural work, a selection of medium-quality fine artist's brushes is important. Imitation sable or nylon work well and are less expensive than real sable or pony hair brushes. Store them in a tube or brush wrap; do not store soft brushes in a pot with the bristles pointing downwards as they will bend.

DUSTING BRUSH

This has endless uses, from dusting items before painting, to colourwashing and dragging. Natural bristle is more flexible and durable. Dusting brushes continue to perform well, even when they begin to wear into a stump.

DRAGGING BRUSH

This is a speciality brush with extra long flexible bristles for creating a fine striped effect. If you have a choice of dragging brush, always go for one with a comfortable handle.

VARNISHING BRUSH

Not essential but such a joy to work with, a varnishing brush looks just like a normal household brush until you turn it to the side and see that it is only about 5mm (⅛in) thick. The bristles are very flexible, hold a lot of varnish or paint and help to feather oil-based paints in particular so that a perfectly smooth paint surface is obtained with minimum effort.

STIPPLING BRUSH

Use a stippling brush for removing brushstrokes and for creating a dotty stippled paint effect. Most decorators use stippling brushes about 5cm (2in) square. Larger stipplers are faster to work with but become heavy as the hours pass. Stippling brushes are expensive and can be replaced at a push with a large emulsion brush from which the loose bristles have been carefully picked out. If you use an emulsion brush be sure to move it around as you work in order to avoid the imprint of the straight edges showing.

HOUSEHOLD BRUSHES

A good selection of general household brushes is the starting point for any decorator. Buy the most expensive you can afford; cheap brushes will shed many hairs and not last long. Look out for a hole in the middle of the bristles which has been filled with a wooden wedge. This will fill with paint and the brush will drip.

WALLPAPER PASTING BRUSH

Use this large brush for smoothing wallpaper into position on a wall. It is wide and comfortable to handle for long periods at a time.

SASH BRUSHES

Originally designed to help with the painting of complicated sash windows, sash brushes are available with pointed or rounded tips. They are perfect for edging and lining, and also for stippling paint on small areas or when control is required. With a little practice you will be able to apply paint in a perfectly straight line by using a sash brush. It may well become an essential part of your decorating kit and reduce your masking tape expenses.

RADIATOR BRUSH

This is a standard household brush attached to a long-angled handle; it is helpful for painting behind radiators and pipework.

CHOOSING BRUSHES

• *Good bristles have split ends, cheap nylon and bad bristles do not. It is easier to achieve a smooth finish with fine, soft bristles.*

• *Always use the narrowest brush you can bear as this will give you greater control and a longer period of time before a brush becomes too heavy.*

Tools

ROLLERS

Use long-pile rollers for textured finishes or uneven surfaces, and short-pile rollers for a smooth finish. A foam roller is useful for a smooth finish with oil-based paints but may bubble or 'orange peel'; work slowly with a well-loaded roller to avoid this. The small rollers sold for gloss paint are a useful addition to any painter's kit as they can be cleaned more easily than larger rollers.

SANDPAPER

Available in different grades, sandpaper is used for rubbing down and smoothing surfaces prior to painting, and for cleaning any drips of paint from a carpet.

ICE CUBE TRAY

Useful as a palette which holds a little sample of many colours at one time; it is easy to hold in one hand at the top of a ladder when painting detailing and murals.

PAINT PADS

These are wonderful speed painters, faster than a brush and smoother than a pile roller. Made from foam with a mohair painting surface, they are available in a wide range of sizes. Paint pads are more economical with paint and much easier to wash than rollers. Work in every direction adjusting the pressure from light to heavy as the pad runs out of paint.

TACK RAGS

These are sold as disposable cloths on a roll, or separately packed. They are lightly impregnated with spirits and oils and are perfect for wiping away dust after sanding a wooden item, prior to priming, painting and varnishing it. The oils and spirits can also help with cleaning paintwork prior to painting but sugar soap should be used if you are going to use a water-based paint.

TOOLS FOR GLAZE WORK

Not all glaze finishes are carried out with the aid of an expensive speciality brush. Plastic bags can be screwed up and used to create a leathery effect, corks can be jabbed in to the glaze for a fossil effect and rags used to create a soft mottled look. Experiment with anything which will not leave lint or fluff in the glaze – try clingfilm or foil and even the side of your fist or your fingertips.

PAINT TRAYS

These are not just for rolling paint, they are also useful for standing open cans of paint in and for mixing small quantities of paint.

DISPOSABLE PAPER PALETTE

Use this for tiny quantities of several colours at one time. The tear-off sheets eliminate any cleaning at the end of the day. Very comfortable to hold for long periods.

PAINT KETTLES

Sturdy and reliable containers for a tin of paint or a glaze mixture. A kettle can be hung from the top of a ladder with a meat hook or the handle. Keep an empty kettle handy for putting wet brushes in. Plastic kettles need not be washed after use and can be re-used after the paint has dried until eventually you throw them away. Steel kettles are more expensive and therefore require more care and cleaning.

MAHL STICK

This is a cane with a soft ball of chamois leather or cloth tied to the end. For high work which requires a very steady hand, hold the mahl stick in your non-painting hand, supporting the cane under your arm. Rest the ball on the wall. You can then rest your painting wrist on the stick and remain steady, even for minute details. You can make a mahl stick by attaching a cut tennis ball to one end of a cane with a large square of chamois leather wrapped over the ball and tied securely to the cane.

Suppliers & Acknowledgements

The following companies supplied paints, wallpapers, furniture and accessories:

Designers Guild
267-77 Kings Road
Chelsea
London SW3 5EN
Tel: 0171-351 5775
Wallpaper, cushions, teddy bear and jug used in lemon and lime room.

The publishers wish to thank the following photographers and organizations for their kind permission to reproduce the photographs in this book on the following pages:
page 6 (bottom) Tom Leighton / Homes and Gardens / Robert Harding; page 7 (top) Christopher Drake / Homes and Gardens / Robert Harding; page 7 (bottom) Simon Kenny / Belle / Arcaid; page 12 Tom Leighton / Homes and Gardens / Robert Harding; page 13 Paul Ryan (Designer Frances Halliday) / International Interiors; page 15 Simon Kenny / Belle / Arcaid.

Franklins
161 Camberwell Road
London SE5
Tel: 0171-703 6429
Antique French bed used in natural room and lemon and lime room

Habitat
Various branches
Tel: 01645 334433 for information
Various accessories

ICI Paints
Wexham Road
Slough
Berkshire SL2 5DS
Tel: 01753 550555
Paints

Ikea
Various branches
Tel: 0181-208 5600 for information
Bedside tables, slatted shoe rack, lantern and rag rug used in Matisse room

Plough Homecraft Company
352-6 Lordship Lane
East Dulwich
London SE22 8LZ
Tel: 0181-693 4785
Decorator's materials

Index

DEDICATION:
For my husband Trevor and my two children Amber and Barnaby, without whom 'I would be lost in space.'

AUTHOR'S ACKNOWLEDGEMENTS
Paintings supplied by Trevor Halliday. Thanks to Tim Imrie and his team for their superb photography, hospitality and for making our time in the studio such fun. Thanks also to Fanny for her amazing ability to find exactly the right thing and then know exactly where to put it. A big thank you to the two Sarahs, Sara Colledge for seeking me out and not giving up, and Sarah Duffin for her support and hard work, which was always done with a smile.

First published in 1999 by Merehurst Limited
Ferry House, 51-57 Lacy Road, Putney, London SW15 1PR

Copyright © 1999 Merehurst Limited

ISBN 185391-633-1

Editor: Heather Dewhurst
Designers: Siân Keogh and Martin Laurie at Axis Design
Photographer: Tim Imrie
Stylist: Fanny Ward
Series concept and Creative Director: Marylouise Brammer
Commissioning Editor: Anna Sanderson
CEO & Publisher: Anne Wilson
International Sales Director: Mark Newman
Colour separation by Bright Arts in Hong Kong
Printed in Singapore by Tien Wah Press